FAITH CLINIC

VOLUME VI

- GRIEF CLINIC EDITION -

STOP ASKING IF I AM OK,
BECAUSE I AM NOT!

*A Grief Clinic Guide For Healing &
Prescriptions For The Brokenhearted.*

DR. PATRICIA S. TANNER

©Copyright 2025

IBG Publications, Inc.

DR. PATRICIA S. TANNER

Published by I.B.G. Publications, Inc., a Power to Wealth Company

Web address: www.ibgpublications.com

admin@ibgpublications.com / 904-419-9810

Copyright, 2025 by Patricia S. Tanner

IBG Publications, Inc., Jacksonville, FL

ISBN: 978-1-956266-94-8

Tanner, Patricia S.
Faith Clinic, Volume VI- Grief Clinic Edition-A Grief Clinic Guide For Healing & Prescriptions For The Brokenhearted

---

All rights reserved. This book, or its parts may not be reproduced in any form, stored in a retrieval system, or transmitted in any form, by any means-electronic, mechanical, photocopy, recording or otherwise, without prior written permission of the publisher or author, except as provided by the United States of America Copyright law.

Printed in the United States of America.

FAITH CLINIC-VOLUME VI-GRIEF CLINIC EDITION

DEDICATION

To every heart silently breaking…
To every tear shed behind closed doors…
To the one who smiles so others won't ask questions…
This book is dedicated to you.

You who have buried loved ones, lost pieces of yourself, or watched dreams die too soon—know that your grief is seen, your pain is real, and your healing is possible. You are not invisible. You are not alone.

As your Faith Doctor, I extend my heart, my prayers, and this healing prescription to walk with you through the valley of grief and into the arms of restoration. May these words remind you that God is still the Great Physician, and His presence is the balm your soul has been craving.

Healing begins here.
One dose at a time.
Welcome to the Faith Clinic.

DR. PATRICIA S. TANNER
The Faith Doctor

DR. PATRICIA S. TANNER

FAITH CLINIC-VOLUME VI-GRIEF CLINIC EDITION

TABLE OF CONTENTS

DEDICATION………………..………..……………….………....3
INTRODUCTION……………………………………….….........7
Why You're Here-The Real Reason You Picked Up This Book

CHAPTER 1:   Grief Isn't Cute-It's Chaos……………….…….…….19

CHAPTER 2:   The Silence After The Funeral…...………..…….…..33

CHAPTER 3:   Time Doesn't Heal-God Does………....................…45

CHAPTER 4:   Angry At God-Yet Still Loved By Him…....…...........57

CHAPTER 5:   Stop With The Platitudes……………..…….…..…67

CHAPTER 6:   When Grief Hits The Body Too………………..…..81

CHAPTER 7:   Faith Feels Flat-And That's Normal……………..…..95

CHAPTER 8:   The Guilt & The What If's…………………..……115

CHAPTER 9:   Healing Doesn't Mean Forgetting………………...125

CHAPTER 10:   Still Breathing-Still Called…………..………….135

EPILOGUE……..………………………………….…..…....143

About The Author…………………..……………………......159
Other Books By The Author……………………………..……161
Contact The Author……………………………………….....175

DR. PATRICIA S. TANNER

FAITH CLINIC-VOLUME VI-GRIEF CLINIC EDITION

INTRODUCTION

WELCOME TO THE GRIEF CLINIC

Why You're Here: The Real Reason You Picked Up This Book

Let's be honest — you didn't grab this book because everything in your life is fine. You didn't flip through these pages because you were bored or casually curious. You're here because something hurt you. Someone you loved is gone. You are grieving, and you're trying to find some sort of compass to navigate the wilderness of loss.

I know that pain — intimately.

When I lost my mother to COVID-19, my world split open. She was strong, vibrant, full of life. One day we were at a doctor's appointment; the next, I was watching her slip away through hospital glass, isolated and sedated. I wasn't prepared — not for the diagnosis, not for the 30-day descent into heartache, not for the moment I had to pray and tell God to take her because I couldn't bear the weight of deciding to pull the plug.

It was a test — of my hope, my mind, my strength, and my faith. And prior to my mother's death, I lost my father to stage four cancer. The two people who nurtured me through life were now both gone. Grief came like a thief, and I had no map. I was walking in darkness, and still, God's voice whispered through the shadows.

This book was born from that journey, and I share it inside my book, *The 30-Days Challenge: I Tested Positive For COVID-19*.

What you're holding isn't just another book — it's a lifeline. It's the result of divine instruction during my darkest season. One evening, in the thick of grief and uncertainty, I fell into what I can only describe as a supernatural trance. When I came to, I had written the outline for what became a healing journal — *30 Days of Grieving: Given By The Inspiration of God*. Both of these books were given by God not just for my healing, but for yours.

He knew that thousands, maybe millions, would walk through the pain of sudden loss without closure, without preparation, and without peace. He knew that many would wrestle with guilt, rage, denial, confusion — and He knew they would need help to find their way back to hope.

So, this *Grief Clinic Edition* of the *Faith Clinic* series was crafted to walk beside you — one honest, scripture-soaked step at a time. You'll see how my faith was tested, how I broke down, how I questioned everything — and how God carried me through.

What You Won't Find Here

This is not a *"pray it away"* manual. It's not a sugary, "they're in a better place" cliché-fest. I won't insult your pain with platitudes. I won't offer quick fixes or shallow timelines. Because grief is not linear — it spirals, pulses, and catches you off guard in the grocery store or in the middle of worship. And that's okay.

I'm not here to rush you. I'm here to sit with you in the ashes, like Jesus did with Mary and Martha when Lazarus died. He knew resurrection was coming, but He still wept. If the Son of God could cry, so can you.

What You Will Find

You'll find rawness, realness, and revival. You'll find permission to feel it all — the numbness, the anger, the relief, the guilt, the laughter through tears. You'll find faith anecdotes — spiritual prescriptions to treat your soul when grief feels like a sickness with no cure. And you'll find a woman who's been through the fire and emerged with scars that still hurt, but also with a testimony that still heals.

This book is for the brave — not because you feel strong, but because you keep showing up anyway. You're not alone. You're not forgotten. You are not faithless because you're grieving. And yes — you can survive this.

Let's take this journey together.

SYMPTOM CHECK:

- Smiling in public, collapsing in private.
- Saying "I'm fine" when the truth is, "I can't breathe."
- Feeling like joy would betray the one you lost.
- Wondering if God left when grief walked in.
- Tired of people asking, *Are you okay?"* because the answer is still *no*.

If you saw yourself in any of those lines, you're in the right place.

💊 FAITH PRESCRIPTION

Take this to heart:

The Lord is close to the brokenhearted and saves those who are crushed in spirit." — **Psalm 34:18 (NIV)**

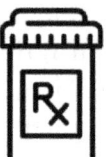

- ✓ Grief will tell you that you're alone. God reminds you He is close.

- ✓ Grief says you're abandoned. God whispers you're carried.

- ✓ Grief screams, "You'll never get through this." God anchors you in truth: you will.

This book isn't here to erase grief. It's here to remind you that grief and grace can coexist — and that healing honors memory, it doesn't erase it.

 SPIRITUAL VITAMIN

Vitamin H: Hope — Take daily.

Say it out loud: *Hope isn't denial. Hope is survival. My breath is proof that God isn't finished with me yet."*

🕊 HOLY SPIRIT CONSULT

Sit with these questions before you dive into the chapters:

FAITH CLINIC-VOLUME VI-GRIEF CLINIC EDITION

- What lie about grief have I been believing? ("I should be over it by now." "I have to be strong for everyone else." "If I cry too much, it means I don't trust God.")

- What is one safe space (person, place, journal) where I can stop pretending and just be real?

- When was the last time I felt God's nearness, even in pain?

Write your answers, cry through them, yell if you need to. God isn't grading your response. He's listening.

 Guided Prayer + Declaration

Prayer:
"God, I don't even know where to start. The pain feels bigger than me. The silence feels louder than me. And sometimes, You feel further than I can reach.

But I choose to believe You are still near. I don't need to fake it — You see the real me. Walk with me through this grief. Sit with me in the numbness. Carry me when I collapse.

Thank You that tears are not weakness — they are prayers in liquid form. In Jesus' name, amen."

Declaration (say it over yourself):

- I am not weak because I grieve.

- I am not faithless because I cry.

- I am not abandoned because I feel broken.

- I am still here, and God is still with me.

📖 Journal Reflection Page

Today's Prompt:

- Write down the last memory of your loved one that made you smile.

_____
_____
_____
_____
_____
_____
_____
_____

- Write the one question you're afraid to ask God about your loss.

_____
_____
_____
_____
_____
_____

FAITH CLINIC-VOLUME VI-GRIEF CLINIC EDITION

_____
_____

- Now, write one truth from scripture that speaks louder than the ache.

_____
_____
_____
_____
_____
_____
_____
_____

Example starter:

"My mom/dad taught me _____.
Today, I honor their memory by _____.
God, even in my grief, I choose to believe _____."

⚕ Faith Clinic Intake Form — Grief Edition

(Because I'm fine" is not a diagnosis)

Patient Name:
_____

DR. PATRICIA S. TANNER

Date of Admission: _____

Loss Being Grieved: _____

1. Presenting Symptom(s):

(Check all that apply — honesty required, no filters)

☐ Random crying episodes in grocery store aisles

☐ Anger at God, people, or walls that didn't do anything wrong

☐ Feeling numb when everyone else expects emotions

☐ Overwhelmed by silence after the funeral

☐ Guilt ("What if I had…?")

☐ Regret over last words or no closure

☐ Exhaustion / "grief brain" / forgetting everything

☐ Pretending I'm okay so people stop asking

☐ Other: _____

2. Severity of Symptoms:

Circle one:
😌 Manageable | 😬 Barely Holding It Together
😰 Falling Apart | 💀 Not Okay At All

3. Coping Mechanisms Currently In Use:

(Be honest — this is between you and God)

- Netflix binging until my eyes cross.
- Scrolling social media for distraction.
- Avoiding people because they say dumb things.
- Church, but with a fake smile.
- Prayer (angry, messy, half-finished).
- Eating my feelings (chocolate should count as communion).
- Writing/journaling.
- Other: _____

4. *Spiritual Vital Signs:* *Check all that apply*

- **Prayer Life:**
  ☐ Nonexistent ☐ Desperate "God, help" ☐ Sporadic
  ☐ Honest but messy ☐ Consistent

- **Faith Status:**
  ☐ Hopeful ☐ Questioning ☐ Angry ☐ Numb
  ☐ Clinging by a thread

- **Support System:**
  ☐ Strong and Present ☐ Small but Steady
  ☐ Inconsistent ☐ Vanished After the Funeral

5. *Misdiagnoses You've Believed:*

(Check all lies you've caught yourself thinking)

☐ "Time heals all wounds."

- ☐ "I should be over this by now."
- ☐ "Crying makes me weak."
- ☐ "God is disappointed in me for grieving too long."
- ☐ "If I have faith, I shouldn't hurt this much."
- ☐ "Nobody cares anymore."
- ☐ Other: _____

6. *Immediate Needs:*

(What you're really craving in this season — no churchy answers required)

- ☐ Presence (someone to just *be* there)
- ☐ Permission (to cry, to scream, to grieve honestly)
- ☐ Rest (physical, emotional, spiritual)
- ☐ Scripture that doesn't feel cliché
- ☐ Assurance that God hasn't left me
- ☐ Space to heal without pressure

Other: _____

7. *Prescribed Treatment Plan:*

Symptoms Identified: _____

FAITH CLINIC-VOLUME VI-GRIEF CLINIC EDITION

Faith Prescription (Scripture):_____

Spiritual Vitamin (Truth to Repeat): _____

Next Appointment With God (Prayer Time):_____

Doctor's Note (Jesus 'Signature):

Blessed are those who mourn, for they will be comforted."
(Matthew 5:4)

DR. PATRICIA S. TANNER

"Grief is the wound no bandage can hide. But faith? Faith is the salve that seeps into the soul when words fall short."

-DR. PATRICIA S. TANNER

FAITH CLINIC-VOLUME VI-GRIEF CLINIC EDITION

Chapter 1

Grief Isn't Cute, It's Chaos

DR. PATRICIA S. TANNER

💬 SYMPTOM:

🩺 EMOTIONAL WHIPLASH

Grief doesn't arrive in neat packages — it crashes in with waves of rage, sorrow, guilt, and numbness all at once. One minute you're silent, the next you're screaming on the inside. It's emotional whiplash — unpredictable, uncontrollable, and deeply unsettling.

Grief isn't orderly, polished, or manageable. It's chaos. One minute you're laughing at a memory, and the next you're choking on tears in the grocery aisle because a box of cereal reminded you of them. Grief makes you unpredictable, inconsistent, and exhausted. It doesn't come in polite doses — it crashes in waves, sometimes when you least expect it, sometimes when you can't handle it.

But the real problem? The world wants grief to look inspirational. People expect you to have a breakdown that's Instagram-worthy — pretty tears, a gentle scripture quote, and a worship song swelling in the background. But grief doesn't look like a Christian movie scene. It looks like swollen eyes, unfinished prayers that sound more like complaints, and mascara that makes you look like you lost a bar fight.

The symptom is clear: grief isn't cute. It's messy, loud, and disruptive. And you feel pressure to make it look prettier than it is.

Grief isn't polite. It doesn't knock on your door and wait for you to tidy up before barging in. It storms into your life like an unwanted guest who drags mud all over your clean floors, throws itself onto your couch, and dares you to do something about it. The problem is

— you can't. You didn't invite grief, but now it's living rent-free in your head, your heart, and even your body.

It's chaos, pure and simple. One moment you're functioning fine, maybe even laughing at a memory, and the next moment you're doubled over in tears because a song shuffled onto your playlist, or you passed their favorite restaurant. Grief doesn't care about timing. It will ambush you in the grocery store, humiliate you in public, and keep you awake at three in the morning when you'd give anything for a few hours of peace.

And here's the kicker: people expect you to make it look pretty. Our culture loves *"inspirational grief."* They want your tears to come with a Bible verse attached, your breakdowns to look like a Hallmark commercial, and your mourning to be wrapped in a bow that makes everyone else comfortable.

But your grief doesn't look like that. It looks like swollen eyes, puffy cheeks, and a pile of tissues that could fill a landfill. It looks like you screaming in your car at a red light. It looks like you sitting in church completely numb while everyone else sings, and you can't even get the words out because your chest feels like it's caving in.

Let's be honest — grief is not social media material. It's not "content." Nobody's posting pictures of their grief brain when they forgot where they put their keys for the tenth time in one day. Nobody's uploading a reel of themselves crying on the kitchen floor because the chair across the table is still empty. Nobody's making daily TikToks about waking up and remembering all over again that your loved one is gone.

Your grief is like whiplash: messy, unpredictable, and anything but inspirational. And yet, somewhere inside you, there's pressure to hide it, clean it up, and make it palatable for everyone else. That pressure to look "okay" when you are not its own kind of pain.

Grief makes you feel like a walking contradiction. You want to be alone, but loneliness is suffocating. You want people around, but their presence can feel overwhelming. You want to talk about it, but you don't want to explain yourself again. You want to forget, but you also don't want to let go. That tension is exhausting. And it leaves you wondering: *Am I broken? Am I doing this wrong?*

No, friend. You're not doing it wrong. This is just what grief looks like. It's not tidy. It's not "cute." It's chaos. And the worst part? Most of the world doesn't know what to do with your chaos, so they rush you to hide it. That's the symptom. You're hurting, but you're also pressured to perform like you're not.

GRIEF CLINIC TOOLKIT

Emotional Whiplash Tool: John 11:35

The Bible doesn't sanitize grief either. It gives us the shortest verse in all of Scripture, and maybe the most profound: *Jesus wept"* **(John 11:35).** The Son of God — who knew He was about to raise Lazarus from the dead — still cried. That's not chaos denied, that's chaos embraced.

What does that tell us? That tears are not weakness, they're worship. If Jesus Himself allowed grief to overwhelm Him in that moment, you don't need to filter yours. If the Son of God didn't hide His sorrow to make people comfortable, neither should you.

Here s the truth: grief is not the opposite of faith. Grief is evidence of love. You cry because it mattered. You broke because it was real.

And God meets you in that breaking — not once you've polished it up, not once you've "moved on," but right in the ugly, chaotic middle.

Here's the truth you need to hear up front: grief doesn't disqualify you from faith — it reveals it. The fact that you are hurting this deeply doesn't mean you're spiritually weak. It means you loved deeply. Grief is the shadow love casts when someone or something precious is torn from us. It's not evidence of faithlessness; it's evidence of connection.

But here's where the teaching must cut through: somewhere along the way, church culture (and honestly, just society in general) gave us the wrong picture of grief. We've been told to tidy it up, wrap it in scripture, and make it palatable for other people. We've been told to move on quickly, to "celebrate their life" with more smiles than tears, to "hold it together" so that everyone else around us feels better. But that's not biblical. That's not honest. That's not healing.

Look at Jesus.

He stood at the tomb of Lazarus, His friend. He knew resurrection power was in His hands. He knew, in just a few moments, He would call Lazarus back to life. And yet… He still wept. He didn't put on a brave face. He didn't stand there with a fake smile and say, "Don't worry, God's got this." He let grief wash over Him.

Why? Because love hurts. Because death is an enemy, not a friend. Because loss wasn't part of God's original design. Jesus knew He was about to reverse that loss, and yet His heart still broke. And if the Son of God Himself felt the sting of grief so deeply that He cried in public, then who told you that your tears make you weak?

The Psalms echo this repeatedly. David, a man after God's own heart, cried out, *"My tears have been my food day and night"*

(**Psalm 42:3**). That doesn't sound like someone who had it all together. That sounds like someone who knew grief was overwhelming — and yet he brought it into the presence of God. That's what made him strong: not the absence of tears, but the willingness to bring them to the throne.

Let's be real: grief feels like chaos because it ***is*** chaos. But God isn't intimidated by your chaos. Remember **Genesis 1:2**? *"The earth was without form and void, and darkness was over the face of the deep. And the Spirit of God was hovering over the waters."*

That's what the Spirit does — He hovers over voids. He doesn't run from darkness; He brings light into it. The same Spirit that hovered over creation hovers over your grief right now.

Here's where faith comes in: faith isn't pretending you're fine. Faith is admitting you're not fine, and still daring to believe God hasn't left you in the rubble.

Faith is ugly crying and saying, "God, I don't understand, but I need You here." Faith is screaming at heaven and trusting God to handle your raw honesty. Faith is showing up, even when you don't feel like it, because deep down you believe God will show up too.

So, the tool for your toolkit is this: grief doesn't mean you're broken beyond repair. Grief means you loved and love always leaves a mark. You're not a bad Christian for falling apart. You're human. And you serve a Savior who fell apart at His friend's tomb, too.

If grief is chaos, then let it be chaos. Just don't let it be chaos alone. Let it be chaos with God in the middle of it. Because the One who wept at Lazarus's tomb still weeps with you now.

FAITH CLINIC-VOLUME VI-GRIEF CLINIC EDITION

FAITH PRESCRIPTION

Psalm 34:18 (NIV): *The Lord is close to the brokenhearted and saves those who are crushed in spirit."*

Doctor s Orders: Take this verse like medicine. Don't just read it — swallow it. Break it down. The Lord isn't far away when you're brokenhearted; He's *closest* then.

Think about that: the very moments you feel most abandoned are the moments He is literally leaning in the nearest.

When your heart feels shattered, you don't need people who throw you clichés. You need a God who gets down in the shards with you.

Psalm 34:18 says He saves those who are crushed in spirit. Not those who are smiling through it. Not those who have it all together. Not those who manage to keep their mascara intact. No — those who are **crushed**. That means your most broken, most chaotic, most overwhelmed moments are the exact qualifications for His closeness.

Take this prescription every morning and every night if needed. Whisper it through your tears. Shout it if you must. Tape it on your fridge, your bathroom mirror, or the dashboard of your car. Let this scripture rewire your brain: grief doesn't push God away — it pulls Him closer.

SPIRITUAL VITAMIN

Daily Dose: *Grief is not weakness. Grief is proof that love mattered."*

This is your vitamin. Take it daily until it dissolves into your spirit. Write it on a sticky note and paste it in your bathroom mirror. Say it when you feel guilty for crying. Say it when someone implies you should "be strong." Say it when you think you're annoying God with your tears.

Grief is not an interruption of life. It's the echo of love that refuses to disappear. If it hurts this much, it's because it mattered that much. Your tears are not wasted — they are seeds God collects (**Psalm 56:8** says He bottles them). And if God bothers to save your tears in a bottle, then He clearly doesn't see them as weakness. He sees them as holy.

So, every day, remind yourself: "I'm not weak for grieving. I'm human. And I'm loved by a God who grieves with me."

HOLY SPIRIT CONSULT

Here's what the Holy Spirit would say if you stopped long enough to breathe and listen:

You don't scare Me with your chaos."

Read that again. Your breakdowns don't make the Spirit back away. Your screaming, your silence, your numbness, your unpredictable emotions — none of it makes Him flinch. The Spirit doesn't hover over clean, well-organized spaces.

The Bible says, *The earth was formless and empty, and darkness covered the deep waters. And the Spirit of God was hovering over the surface of the waters"* (**Genesis 1:2, NLT**). That means His specialty is chaos. He broods over disorder. He sits in the darkness until light breaks through.

So why do you believe the lie that you need to "get it together" before you can feel Him? That's not the gospel. The Spirit has always shown up where life looks most undone. He hovered at creation. He descended at Jesus 'baptism. He came like fire in Acts when the disciples were confused and afraid. And He's hovering over your grief now.

The consult is simple: stop thinking your chaos is too much for God. It's exactly where He does His best work.

🙏 Guided Prayer + Declarations

Prayer
"God, I m sitting here in the middle of chaos, and honestly, I don t even have the words for this pain. My grief feels bigger than me. It feels bigger than my strength, my understanding, and even my faith sometimes.

But thank You that it is not bigger than You. Thank You that You are near to the brokenhearted — and that means You are near to me right now.

Help me stop trying to tidy up my pain before I bring it to You. Teach me to be honest in my grief, like Jesus was at Lazarus s tomb. Hold me in my tears, my questions, my silence, and my chaos. Amen."

Declarations (say these out loud — even through tears):

- I declare that my tears are not a sign of weakness but proof of love.

- I declare that God is near to me in my brokenness, not far away.

- I declare that the Holy Spirit hovers over my chaos, bringing light and order.

- I declare that my grief is not too much for God to handle.
- I declare that healing does not require pretending.

📝 Journal + Reflection Page

Take this section seriously — it's your turn to process:

1. **Describe your grief in real, unfiltered terms.** Not the polite version you give people when they ask if you're okay, but the actual messy version. What does it look like on your hardest days?

   _____
   _____
   _____
   _____
   _____
   _____
   _____
   _____

2. **Where have you felt pressure to make your grief "look better" for others?** Who has made you feel like you must be strong, and how has that affected your healing?

   _____
   _____
   _____

3. **Think about John 11:35 — "Jesus wept."** Why do you think Jesus cried even though He knew resurrection was coming? What does that say about His compassion for you?

4. **Write a prayer or letter to God** that expresses exactly how your grief feels right now — even if it sounds angry, confused, or unfinished. Don't censor yourself.

_____

_____

_____

_____

_____

_____

_____

_____

_____

_____

5. **Reflection Question:** How might grief become less of a secret shame and more of a place where you meet God honestly?

_____

_____

_____

_____

_____

Closing Note

Grief isn't cute. It's chaos. But that chaos is not a sign that you've lost your faith — it's a sign that you've loved deeply, and that love matters enough to leave a mark. Don't sanitize it. Don't perform it. Don't rush it. Let it be messy, loud, confusing, and holy.

Because here s the truth: God doesn't hover over your polished performances. He hovers over your chaos. And He's here now.

- I declare that grief does not disqualify me from God's love.
- I declare that tears are not weaknesses, they are worship.
- I declare that God is near to me, even in the middle of chaos.
- I declare that my pain has a place in God's presence.

"Grief is not a delicate emotion—it's a full-body storm. Don't minimize your pain to make others comfortable. God can handle your chaos."

-DR. PATRICIA S. TANNER

FAITH CLINIC-VOLUME VI-GRIEF CLINIC EDITION

Chapter 2

The Silence After The Funeral

DR. PATRICIA S. TANNER

SYMPTOM:

NUMBNESS IN THE NOISE OF QUIET

When the crowds disappear and the caskets are closed, silence becomes deafening. You feel the weight of absence in every empty chair and quiet room. The world moves on, but you're suspended in stillness — where the loudest sound is your aching heart.

The funeral ends, the casseroles stop arriving, and suddenly the phone doesn't ring as often. In those first days, everyone checked on you. People texted, dropped off food, sent flowers, and filled the house with noise. But now? Quiet. Too quiet. It's the silence after the funeral that hurts the most.

Because here's the truth: after the crowd goes home, you're left staring at the empty chair, scrolling through old texts, or hearing echoes of a voice that isn't there anymore. Everyone else goes back to normal life — back to their routines, their jobs, their schedules — but you? You're stuck in the slow-motion wreckage of your loss. The world moves forward, but you're still picking up pieces.

That silence is suffocating. It's not just the absence of people; it's the absence of distraction. And in that absence, grief gets louder. The tears you held back when the house was full now come crashing down in the quiet. And the truth that nobody wants to say out loud is this: the silence after the funeral feels like abandonment. Like everyone forgot the world just ended for you.

The truth no one really warns you about when you're grieving is this: the funeral is not the hardest part. People assume that the day you lay your loved one to rest is the peak of your pain, the ultimate breaking point, the mountain of sorrow. But what really breaks you is what comes after. It's silence. The suffocating, ear-splitting silence that creeps in once the service is over, the phone calls stop, and the crowd of people fades back into their regular lives.

The days immediately following a loss are often filled with activity — frantic, unwanted, overwhelming activity. There are phone calls to make, clothes to pick out for the service, flowers to order, eulogies to write, and visitors dropping by. People come with tears, hugs, and sympathy. They tell stories, share memories, and try to make you laugh between sobs. The house is full. The phone is buzzing. Cards are piling up on the counter. You're exhausted, but you're not alone.

And then — the funeral ends.

Suddenly, the world goes quiet. People go back to work. Their kids still need rides to soccer practice. Their lives didn't stop, even though yours did. Slowly, the texts become less frequent. The calls fade. The fridge is no longer stocked with donated casseroles. The house empties. And you're left sitting in a chair staring at a space that feels way too large without the one you lost.

That silence is louder than the funeral ever was.

Here's the cruel reality of grief: for everyone else, the funeral is closure. It's their goodbye. But for you, the one left behind, the funeral isn't closure — it's the beginning. It's the first day of the rest of your life without them. And nobody prepares you for how deafening that beginning is.

The silence after the funeral has layers.

It's not just the silence of your phone, though that stings — the "*thinking of you*" texts taper off, the awkward check-ins vanish, and the world assumes you're doing fine because you didn't post another crying selfie. It's not just the silence of an empty house, though that's brutal — the quiet at night when the TV isn't enough, or the stillness in the morning when you expect to hear their voice. It's not even just the silence of people avoiding your grief because they don't know what to say anymore.

 It's the silence inside of you. The silence where their laughter used to live. The silence where their presence used to comfort you. The silence of a voice you'll never hear again, except maybe in a dream. That silence is soul-crushing.

And the worst part? Everyone else seems to forget. To them, time keeps marching. Birthdays are still celebrated, holidays are still coming, Monday mornings are still dreaded. But for you, the silence has no expiration date. You're still here, staring at the empty chair, replaying the last conversation, aching for something you can't get back. You're still in the valley when everyone else climbed out weeks ago.

That's the symptom: silence after the funeral is not relief. It's not peace. It's not closure. It's loneliness magnified, abandonment amplified, and grief intensified. And it convinces you of a dangerous lie — that maybe your grief is invisible now, maybe nobody remembers, maybe you're alone in this.

💼 GRIEF CLINIC TOOLKIT 💼

Tool To Fight Quietness: Job 19:14

The Bible doesn't pretend that loneliness after loss isn't real. In **Job 19:14**, Job laments, *My relatives have gone away; my closest friends have forgotten me."* That verse could've been written yesterday by anyone who's walked through grief. Because that's exactly what happens — people mean well, but they move on. Their lives keep rolling while yours feels paused.

But here's the truth hidden in that pain: people may forget, but God doesn't. He doesn't abandon you after the "event" is over. In fact, Scripture tells us He is *a man of sorrows, acquainted with grief"* (**Isaiah 53:3**). That means your silence isn't empty — it's sacred. Because in the space where others disappear, God's presence becomes undeniable.

Think about Elijah in **1 Kings 19**. He ran into the wilderness, exhausted, alone, and grieving. He wanted to give up entirely. But it was there — in silence, not in noise — that God showed up. Not in the wind, not in the earthquake, not in the fire. God came in a gentle whisper. Sometimes it's not until the people leave and the silence takes over that you discover God's whisper in a way you couldn't before.

So yes, the silence after the funeral hurts. But silence isn't proof of abandonment. It's the stage God uses to remind you that His presence doesn't vanish when the crowd does.

The silence after the funeral may feel like abandonment, but Scripture shows us it's a setup for God's presence. While people move on, God moves in. He doesn't vanish when the casseroles stop. He doesn't fade when the phone grows quiet. He's not one of the "well-meaning friends" who disappears after the service. In fact, silence is often the very place where He does His deepest work.

Job said it bluntly: *"My relatives have gone away; my closest friends have forgotten me"* (**Job 19:14**). That wasn't poetic exaggeration. That was lived grief. Job knew what it felt like to be surrounded in the beginning — when tragedy was fresh, everyone showed up. But as time went on, they scattered. Sound familiar? Job's pain wasn't just in losing everything he loved — it was in realizing the people around him couldn't carry that grief with him long-term.

Here's the tool hidden inside Job's cry: people will forget, but God won't. Your grief is not invisible to Him.

Psalm 56:8 says, *"You keep track of all my sorrows. You have collected all my tears in your bottle. You have recorded each one in your book."* Let that sink in. Every tear. Every sigh. Every 3 a.m. breakdown. Every empty morning. God hasn't missed a single one. Others may have moved on, but God is keeping record — not because He's cold and distant, but because He cares enough to count your cries.

Let's reflect on the life of Elijah again.

In **1 Kings 19**, after experiencing public victory on Mount Carmel, Elijah collapsed in private despair. He ran into the wilderness, overwhelmed and done with life. He even prayed for death. Alone, silent, broken — sound familiar? And it was there, not in the noise, not in the public gatherings, not in the chaos of the crowds, that God came to him. Not in the wind, not in the earthquake, not in the fire — but in a gentle whisper. God showed Elijah that His presence isn't always in the noise of others. Sometimes His presence is clearest in the silence.

That's what the silence after the funeral is for you. Yes, it hurts. Yes, it feels like abandonment. But silence is not absence. Silence is often the stage God uses to whisper truths you couldn't hear any other way.

Like Elijah, Jesus is not allergic to sorrow. He doesn't keep His distance when you're crying alone in your room. He is well-acquainted with grief — He's walked its roads, He's felt its silence,

He's lived its weight. And He doesn't just sympathize; He sits with you. That's what makes His presence in your silence different from anyone else's — He isn't uncomfortable with it. He isn't rushing you. He isn't telling you to move on. He's whispering, *"I'm still here. I'm not going anywhere. Even if the world forgets, I don't."*

Here's the tool for your kit: the silence after the funeral is painful, but it isn't purposeless. It strips away the noise of people's words, the distraction of busyness, and the comfort of routines so that you can finally hear the One voice that never fades. Everyone else may forget. But God records every tear, sits with every silence, and whispers through every lonely night: *"I will never leave you nor forsake you"* (**Deuteronomy 31:6**).

FAITH PRESCRIPTION

Deuteronomy 31:6 (NIV): *Be strong and courageous. Do not be afraid or terrified because of them, for the Lord your God goes with you; He will never leave you nor forsake you."*

Doctor s Orders: You may feel left behind, but you are not left alone. God doesn't send sympathy cards — He sends Himself. When others disappear, He is the constant that remains. When the silence screams, His presence still speaks.

This prescription is not about "being strong" in the way culture defines strength — smiling when you're crumbling or pretending you're okay when you're not. Strength here means refusing to believe the lie that silence equals abandonment. It means clinging to the truth that God is with you in the stillness.

Take this verse every morning like medicine. Repeat it when your phone doesn't ring. Repeat it when the house feels empty. Repeat it when you start wondering if anyone still remembers your pain. God is not like people. He does not leave when the flowers wilt and the food runs out. He stays. Always.

SPIRITUAL VITAMIN

Daily Dose: *Silence is not abandonment. It's space for God's whisper."*

This is your vitamin — take it every time the silence feels unbearable. The world interprets quiet as absence. But in God's kingdom, silence is often invitation. It's the place where you hear what you couldn't hear over the noise.

Think about Elijah's story again. The wind, the earthquake, the fire — all dramatic, all loud, all attention-grabbing. But God wasn't in them. He was in the whisper. That means if you only look for God in the noise — in the crowd, in the busyness, in the activity — you'll miss Him when He shows up quietly in your living room at midnight.

Every time silence makes you anxious, swallow this truth: God's whisper is worth the quiet.

Guided Prayer + Declarations

Prayer
"God, the silence after the funeral hurts more than I expected. The phone doesn't ring. The meals stopped. People have gone back to their lives, but mine feels like it ended.

Thank You that You don't leave me in the silence. Thank You that You don't forget me or rush me. Help me to hear Your whisper when the quiet gets loud. Remind me that silence is not abandonment. Fill this house, this heart, and this silence with Your presence. Amen."

FAITH CLINIC-VOLUME VI-GRIEF CLINIC EDITION

Declarations (say these out loud — even through tears):

- I declare that the silence after the funeral does not mean I am forgotten.

- I declare that God is with me, even when people are not.

- I declare that my grief is not on a timeline.

- I declare that the Holy Spirit speaks in whispers I will learn to hear.

- I declare that silence is not the end — it's the place where God begins again.

📖 Journal + Reflection Page

Take time to sit with these prompts — let them guide you into honesty:

1. **How has the silence after your loss felt to you?** Describe it in detail — not the polished version, but the raw reality.

   _____
   _____
   _____
   _____
   _____

2. **Who showed up for you when you needed them most?** Who drifted away? Write about how both impacted your healing.

3. **In what ways has silence been painful?** In what ways might God want to use it for healing?

4. **Read 1 Kings 19:11–12. Reflect on why God chose to reveal Himself to Elijah in a whisper instead of in the dramatic displays.** What does that mean for your own silence?

FAITH CLINIC-VOLUME VI-GRIEF CLINIC EDITION

_____

_____

5. **Write down a moment when you sensed God's presence in the quiet — even if it was small.** What did it mean to you?

_____

_____

_____

_____

_____

Closing Note

The silence after the funeral is real, raw, and crushing. It feels like abandonment. It feels like nobody remembers your pain. But silence is not absence. It is space — painful, yes, but holy — where God whispers truths you can't hear anywhere else.

Everyone else may go back to their normal. But God will not. He will sit with you in the empty spaces, whisper in the quiet, and remind you daily: *You are not forgotten. You are not alone. I am still here."*

"Grief doesn't end at the gravesite. It echoes in the silence that follows, in the empty chairs and unanswered calls. But even in the quiet, God leans in."

-DR. PATRICIA S. TANNER

FAITH CLINIC-VOLUME VI-GRIEF CLINIC EDITION

Chapter 3

Time Doesn't Heal-God Does

DR. PATRICIA S. TANNER

⚠ SYMPTOM

🩺 RESENTMENT TOWARD THE CALENDAR

Each passing day feels like a betrayal. You're told that time should heal you, but instead, the ticking clock only deepens the wound. Anniversaries become dread-filled reminders, and healing seems distant — because your heart knows it's not time, but God, who holds the cure.

If you've been grieving for more than a few weeks, you've probably already heard this phrase at least once: *Don t worry, time heals all wounds."* And if you're honest, you probably wanted to roll your eyes so hard they got stuck in the back of your head. Because here's the truth — time doesn't heal. It just passes. It doesn't stitch wounds back together. It doesn't fill empty chairs. It doesn't erase birthdays, anniversaries, or the ache of missing someone who's not coming back.

Time doesn't heal; it only gives distance. And distance can make you forget details, yes, but it doesn't take away the pain. Ask anyone who lost a parent 20 years ago. Ask someone who buried a child decades back. The pain doesn't vanish. It changes shape, it may soften in some areas, it may not suffocate the same way, but it doesn't *"go away"* just because a calendar flipped.

The symptom here is the pressure society puts on you to get "better" as time goes on. At first, people check in every day. Then once a week. Then once a month. Then they stop altogether, because *surely* by now you've "moved on." People assume that grief has an expiration date, and when you don't meet it, you feel like a failure.

Like your grief is abnormal. Like you're dragging something dead around that you should've buried with your loved one.

But grief doesn't work like that. It doesn't obey clocks or calendars. It's not a wound that simply scabs over after enough time has passed. It's more like a scar — always there, tender when pressed, faded maybe, but never erased.

And yet the culture around us insists on rushing the process. They want grief to be a short-term project. They want to say the right things, hug you at the funeral, bring your favorite dish, then wipe their hands clean and say, "We did our part." Weeks later, when you're still struggling to get out of bed, they don't know what to do with you anymore. That's because people want your grief to follow their timeline, not yours.

The symptom is this: you feel guilty for still hurting because everyone else thinks you should be done by now. You find yourself saying things like, "I know it's been months, I should be okay…" or "I don't want to keep bringing it up, people are probably tired of hearing about it." You start silencing your grief to make others comfortable.

But suppressing grief doesn't heal it — it buries it alive. And buried grief doesn't disappear; it rots, spreads, and poisons everything else. That's why this idea that "time heals all wounds" is not just untrue — it's dangerous. It convinces you to stop talking, stop processing, and stop being honest. And the longer you fake being okay, the harder it becomes to ever be real again.

Grief on a timeline is a lie. It convinces you that if you're still crying after six months, something's wrong with you. If you feel triggered by a memory two years later, you're weak. That if you still miss them decades down the road, you're "stuck." But let's tell the truth here: missing someone you loved doesn't expire. Love doesn't expire. And because of that, grief doesn't either.

Time doesn't heal wounds. If anything, sometimes time makes them ache more. Because as time goes on, more milestones pass without them. More moments happen where you look around and think, *They should be here for this."* And that realization can hit harder years later than it did in the beginning. Time doesn't fix that — it magnifies it.

So, here s the symptom: you're pressured to believe that your grief should've healed by now. That because time has passed, you should be better. But you're not. And that's not because you're broken — it's because time isn't the healer.

GRIEF CLINIC TOOLKIT

Tool For Calendar Movement: Ecclesiastes 3

If time doesn't heal, then who does? The answer is woven all through Scripture: God Himself. Healing is not the job of clocks or calendars. Healing belongs to the One who holds eternity.

Ecclesiastes 3 says, *There is a time for everything, and a season for every activity under the heavens… a time to weep and a time to laugh, a time to mourn and a time to dance."*

Notice what it doesn t say: "Time heals your mourning." No — it says mourning has a season. And who holds seasons? God. Seasons don't change because of time; they change because God shifts them. You can sit in winter for years, but when God says spring, it comes.

Psalm 147:3 declares, *He heals the brokenhearted and binds up their wounds."* That's not a job given to days, months, or years.

That's God's job. He binds wounds. He stitches hearts. He comforts the crushed. Healing is an act of His presence, not the passage of time.

We see this truth in the life of David. In **2 Samuel 12**, after David's child died, Scripture says he wept, fasted, and prayed while the child was alive. But once the child died, he got up, washed himself, worshiped, and ate. Why? Because he understood something we often miss — healing doesn't come by waiting long enough. Healing comes by encountering God in the loss. David wasn't suddenly "okay" because enough hours passed. He was sustained because he turned to God in the aftermath.

That's the difference: time numbs; God heals. Time creates distance; God creates restoration. Time says, "move on"; God says "come close."

And let's be real: some wounds time can't even touch. The death of a spouse. The loss of a child. The unexpected phone call at midnight. Time may dull the sharpness, but the gap remains. What fills that gap isn't years passing — it's God stepping in with His presence. It's Him saying, *I know this wound. I carried wounds too. I still carry scars."* (**John 20:27**).

That's why your grief doesn't mean you lack faith. It means you need a Healer. And the only true Healer is God. He doesn't put a stopwatch on your sorrow. He doesn't scold you for "still being sad." He sits with you, bottles your tears, and heals piece by piece. Healing in God's presence is not linear, it's *layered*. Sometimes He heals loneliness first. Sometimes anger. Sometimes guilt. And sometimes He just holds you in the ache until you can breathe again. That's healing, too.

So, here's the tool for your kit: **time doesn't heal — God does.** Don't wait for the calendar to fix you. Don't bury your grief because you're "taking too long." Run to the One who heals the brokenhearted. Because He's not looking at His watch; He's looking at you.

FAITH PRESCRIPTION

Psalm 147:3 (NIV): *He heals the brokenhearted and binds up their wounds."*

Doctor's Orders: This verse is not a greeting card slogan. It's a prescription. And like any prescription, it doesn't work if you don't take it. The problem is, too many of us have been swallowing the wrong pill. We've been trying to medicate our grief with *time*.

We've been told, "Just give it a year. It'll get better." So, we circle dates on calendars, hoping that flipping a page will flip our pain. But the truth is, days don't stitch wounds. Months don't close scars. Years don't breathe peace into hollow spaces. God does.

Think about what this verse says. *He heals the brokenhearted."* Who's the He? Not time. Not closure. Not human pep talks. The 'He' is the Great Physician. He doesn't stand at a distance and prescribe healing like a doctor scribbles something on a pad and leaves you to fill it. No — He personally binds wounds.

That word "bind" is intimate. It means He gets close enough to see where you're torn open. He touches the bleeding parts. He wraps His own hands around the pieces of your broken heart and holds them together until the bleeding slows.

When you're told "time heals," what you're really being told is "Wait it out. Ignore it until it gets dull." But God doesn't call you to numbness. He calls you to healing. And healing isn't passive. Healing requires His touch.

Here's the prescription: Stop waiting on calendars and start leaning on Christ. Take **Psalm 147:3** like medicine every single day. When you wake up and still feel the weight of grief, whisper it: *He heals the brokenhearted. He binds up their wounds."* When someone asks if you're better yet, remind yourself: "God is still binding me." When you feel ashamed for not moving on fast enough, remember: "Healing is not timed — it's tended."

Dosage: Take this verse in the morning, at night, and whenever you feel like the wound is splitting open again. Because the truth is, God is the Healer, not time.

💊 SPIRITUAL VITAMIN

Daily Dose: *Time numbs; God heals."*

This is your spiritual multivitamin. Take it with water, coffee, tears, or chocolate — whatever works. Because this truth will keep you sane when everyone else keeps prescribing you "more time."

Think about the difference: numbing versus healing. Time numbs. It dulls the sharpness. It creates distance from the immediate moment of loss. Yes, it's true — the funeral-day pain doesn't feel the same two years later.

But here's the catch: numbing isn't healing. If you've ever had dental work done, you know what numbing feels like. It masks the pain temporarily, but the root problem is still there. And the moment the numbing wears off, the ache reminds you the work isn't finished. That's exactly what "time heals" does. It tricks you into thinking you're fine… until the anniversary date hits, or the song plays, or the empty chair stares back at you. Then you realize nothing was ever healed — it was just muted.

God heals differently. He doesn't numb you; He restores you. His healing is not about forgetting — it's about making it possible to live without bleeding every time the wound is touched. He doesn't erase memories; He gives you grace to carry them without collapsing. He doesn't dull the love you had; He teaches you how to let that love shape your present without destroying your future.

Vitamin - Swallow it daily: Don't settle for numbness. Don't confuse the quieting of pain with the curing of pain. Real healing doesn't come with clocks and calendars. It comes with Christ.

HOLY SPIRIT CONSULT

Imagine this moment like you're sitting in the exam room, and the Holy Spirit pulls up a chair. He looks you in the eyes and says:

I m not rushing you. Stop rushing yourself."

That's the consultation.

Because here s the thing: grief is not a timed test, and you're not failing because you're still crying months or years later. The world puts grief on a stopwatch. Six months? Acceptable. A year? Understandable. Two years? Now you're making people uncomfortable. But the Spirit doesn't measure your healing in hours. He measures it in honesty.

The Holy Spirit specializes in what you can't see happening beneath the surface. Sometimes He's healing you in ways you don't even recognize. He's giving you strength to get out of bed when you thought you couldn't. He's softening your heart so you can laugh again without guilt. He's teaching you to pray differently — less polished, more real. These are signs of healing. And none of it is rushed.

The consult is this: stop letting other people's silence trick you into thinking God is silent. Stop letting their impatience make you think God is impatient. He isn't. He's the Comforter, not the Timekeeper. He doesn't say, "Move on." He says, "Lean in."

So, when the pressure builds, hear Him whisper: *You are not behind. You are not weak. You are not late. You are healing — and I m still here."*

 Guided Prayer + Declarations

Prayer
"God, I ve been told that time heals all wounds, but I know that s not true. Time has passed, but my heart still aches. My mind still wanders about what I lost. My soul still feels cracked.

Thank You that You are not watching a calendar to measure my progress. Thank You that You are the Healer, the One who binds wounds and restores broken hearts. I give You this wound again today. Stitch it. Hold it. Heal it in Your way, not mine. Amen."

Declarations (say these out loud):

- I declare that time does not heal me — God does.

- I declare that my healing is not on a human timeline.

- I declare that my wounds are in the hands of the Great Physician.

- I declare that scars do not mean failure; they mean survival.

- I declare that God is binding my heart even as I grieve.

📝 Journal + Reflection Page

Take time to write through these prompts — they'll help you face the lie of "time heals" and lean into the truth:

1. **When has someone told you that "time heals all wounds?"** How did it make you feel in that moment?

   _____
   _____
   _____
   _____
   _____
   _____

2. **Think about a loss you or someone you know experienced years ago.** Did time erase it, or is it still present in some way? What does that show you?

   _____
   _____
   _____
   _____
   _____
   _____

3. **Read Psalm 147:3 again slowly. Write down what it means for God Himself to "bind up your wounds."**

4. **In what ways are you waiting on time to fix something God is asking you to bring to Him?**

5. **Write a short prayer giving God permission to heal you beyond the limits of time.** Be honest — what do you want Him to touch first?

Closing Note

The lie says: *Give it time, and you'll get better."* The truth says: *Give it to God, and He will heal you."*

Time doesn't erase empty chairs. Time doesn't fill silent rooms. Time doesn't stop the tears that sneak up on anniversaries. But God? God meets you in every one of those moments. He heals, He binds, He restores. He doesn't rush you, and He doesn't abandon you.

Stop waiting on calendars. Lean into Christ. Because healing isn't measured in hours passed — it's measured in His presence held.

FAITH CLINIC-VOLUME VI-GRIEF CLINIC EDITION

Chapter 4

Angry At God-And Still Loved By Him

DR. PATRICIA S. TANNER

⚠ SYMPTOM:

🩺 BITTERNESS WRAPPED IN SILENCE

You feel abandoned by the very God you once trusted. Your prayers have quieted, not because you lack faith, but because you're wrestling with disappointment in the One who could have stopped the loss. You bottle your rage, afraid to admit it—yet your silence is soaked in unshed tears and unspoken questions.

Nobody likes to admit this out loud, especially in church circles, but grief often comes with anger — and not just anger at circumstances, doctors, or people who said the wrong thing. Real anger at God. The kind of anger you don't want to write in your prayer journal. The kind of rage that makes you feel like maybe lightning will strike if you say it out loud.

But here's the truth: when you've buried someone you love, or when loss rips through your life like a storm you didn't see coming, you can't help but ask the burning question: *Why, God?"* Why didn't You heal them? Why didn't You prevent this? Why didn't You intervene? Why them? Why now? Why me?

And when those "why" questions have no answers, anger builds.

It starts subtly. Maybe you stop praying as often. Maybe you avoid worship songs because they feel fake when your heart is shattered. Maybe you show up to church but check out emotionally because you don't want to hear another sermon about God's goodness when you're not convinced He showed up for you. The anger simmers quietly, but it's there.

FAITH CLINIC-VOLUME VI-GRIEF CLINIC EDITION

Other times, it's not subtle at all. It's loud. It's yelling in the car. It's crying into your pillow and saying, *God, where were You?"* It's pacing the floor at night because you can't reconcile His promises with your pain. It's throwing scriptures back at Him like accusations.

And here s the symptom: anger at God makes you feel conflicted. On one hand, you love Him. On the other, you feel betrayed by Him. You want to draw close, but you also want to slam the door. You crave His comfort, but you're furious at His choices. It's a messy tension nobody prepares you for.

What makes this worse is how people react to your anger. Most folks don't know what to do with someone who's mad at God. They tell you things like, *Don t question Him."* Or, *That s dangerous territory."* Or, *You just need to trust more."* Their words don't help — they shame. And now you're not only angry at God, but you're also ashamed for being angry at Him in the first place.

So, you keep it inside. You plaster a polite smile in public. You nod at church when people say, "God is good." But inside? Inside, you're boiling.

Here's the messy truth nobody wants to say: grief can make you mad at God. It's not polite. It's not inspirational. But it's real. And bottling that anger doesn't make it holy; it makes it toxic.

That s the symptom: you're angry at God, but you don't know if you're "allowed" to be. You bury it under guilt, but the resentment grows. You want to trust Him, but you don't trust how He handled your loss. And that unspoken anger eats at your faith like termites in the foundation.

DR. PATRICIA S. TANNER

💼 GRIEF CLINIC TOOLKIT 💼

<u>*Tool For Silent Bitterness*</u>: Psalm 34:18

Now let's expose the truth behind the symptom: anger at God does not make Him stop loving you. The Bible is full of people who got angry at God — and God didn't strike them down. In fact, some of them are celebrated as heroes of faith.

Take Job.

He lost everything — his children, his health, his livelihood. And he did not sit quietly with a fake smile. He raged. He cursed the day he was born (**Job 3:1**). He accused God of targeting him unfairly (**Job 7:17-20**). He shouted his questions into the sky. And God? He didn't kill Job for his honesty. He engaged him. He listened. He responded.

Or take David. Read the Psalms closely and you'll find raw anger woven through them. In **Psalm 13**, he cries, *How long, Lord? Will you forget me forever? How long will you hide your face from me?"* That's not polite Sunday-school prayer. That's gut-level honesty. And God still called David a man after His own heart.

Even Jeremiah, the "weeping prophet," once shouted at God, *You deceived me, Lord, and I was deceived"* (**Jeremiah 20:7**). Imagine saying that to God — "You tricked me." Bold, almost offensive honesty. And yet God didn't abandon Jeremiah.

Here s the teaching: God can handle your anger. He would rather have your honest rage than your fake reverence. Pretending doesn't heal you. Pouring out your raw feelings does.

Why? Because anger at God is often rooted in pain, not rebellion. It's not that you hate Him — it's that you don't understand Him. You're hurting, and anger is how your heart expresses the ache. God sees that. He knows the difference between defiance and despair.

Psalm 34:18 says, *The Lord is close to the brokenhearted and saves those who are crushed in spirit."* It does not say, "The Lord is close to the people who never get mad at Him." It says He's close to the broken. That includes the angry.

Jesus Himself got angry in grief. When Lazarus died, Scripture says He was *deeply moved in spirit and troubled"* (**John 11:33**). The Greek word there implies indignation, even anger. He wept, yes, but He also burned with holy frustration at death itself. Anger in grief is not unholy — it's human.

Here s the truth: being angry at God doesn't disqualify you from His love. In fact, your honesty may be the very thing that draws you closer to Him. Because intimacy with God is not built on pretending — it's built on truth. And sometimes the truest prayer you can pray is, *"God, I m mad at You."*

FAITH PRESCRIPTION

Psalm 13:1–2 (NIV): *How long, Lord? Will you forget me forever? How long will you hide your face from me? How long must I wrestle with my thoughts and day after day have sorrow in my heart?"*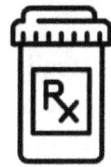

Doctor s Orders: If David — the man after God's own heart — could pray like this, then so can you.

Prescription: stop censoring your grief in prayer. Take this verse as permission to wrestle with God out loud. Don't just whisper polite thank-you's when your chest is caving in with sorrow. Don't choke on memorized churchy prayers that you don't mean. Take **Psalm 13** as your spiritual script and say exactly what you feel.

David wasn't punished for asking "How long, Lord?" He was loved through it. His words weren't lightning bait; they were intimacy. Because God doesn't heal fake wounds — He heals the ones you expose. And if that means your prayers sound angry, disappointed, or even accusatory, so be it. They're still prayers. They're still conversations. And silence is more dangerous to your soul than shouting.

Second Rx: pray honestly, even when it's ugly. Write it, scream it, whisper it, cry it. Don't polish it up for heaven. God's shoulders are broad enough to carry your rage.

💊 SPIRITUAL VITAMIN

Daily Dose: *My anger doesn't scare God. My honesty invites Him."*

Take this vitamin daily, especially on the mornings you feel guilty for still being mad. Repeat it until it sinks in. Your anger does not frighten God, offend Him, or make Him withdraw from you. He is not like people who ghost you when you're "too much." He doesn't leave the room because your emotions are loud.

Instead, your honesty is what pulls Him closer. Think about it: if David's brutally raw psalms are included in Scripture for all eternity, then clearly God values honesty over performance. He didn't censor David's complaints; He canonized them. That means your anger, expressed truthfully before Him, is still worship. Yes — even shouting is worship if it's directed at the God who can handle it.

Take this vitamin with your grief each day. Anger is not poison when it's confessed; it's only poison when it's buried. Let honesty be the open door for God to walk into your pain.

FAITH CLINIC-VOLUME VI-GRIEF CLINIC EDITION

HOLY SPIRIT CONSULT

Picture yourself sitting in the Faith Clinic exam room, head down, ashamed of how furious you've been with God. The Holy Spirit leans in, looks you in the eye, and says:

I'd rather you yell at Me than walk away from Me."

That's the consultation.

The Spirit is not intimidated by your rage. He knows that behind your anger is heartbreak, and behind your heartbreak is love. Your fury doesn't drive Him away — your silence does. He is the Comforter, not the critic. His role isn't to shame you into politeness but to stay with you through the storm until you can breathe again.

The Spirit reminds you: *I know why you're mad. I was there when the loss happened. I saw it. I wept too. You're not crazy for being angry — you're human. And I'm not walking away."*

Stop holding it in. Stop treating your anger like it disqualifies you from His presence. The consult is clear: you can be angry at God and still be in God. He hasn't left you — not for a second.

Guided Prayer + Declarations

Prayer
"God, I don't always know how to say this without guilt, but I'm angry. Angry at what happened. Angry at what You didn't stop. I am angry that my life feels shattered.

Thank You that You don't punish me for this honesty. Thank You that You love me even in the middle of my questions. Teach me to bring my anger to You instead of burying it. Amen."

Declarations

- I declare that God loves me even when I'm angry.
- I declare that honesty is not rebellion; it's intimacy.
- I declare that my grief can include rage, and God can handle it.
- I declare that silence is more dangerous than shouting.

 Journal + Reflection Page

Reflect on these prompts:

1. **What moments in your grief have made you most angry at God?** Write them down without editing.

    _____
    _____
    _____
    _____
    _____
    _____
    _____
    _____
    _____

2. **What have you felt too guilty to admit to Him out loud?**

    _____
    _____

3. Read Psalm 13. What stands out to you about David's honesty?

4. How does knowing God can handle your anger change the way you pray?

5. Write your own raw "Psalm of anger" to God — no filters.

📝 Closing Note

Anger at God doesn't mean you've lost your faith. It means your heart is raw, wounded, and desperate for answers. And God would rather sit with your fury than your faking.

He's not afraid of your rage. He's not walking away from your honesty. You can be angry at Him — and still be loved by Him. *Always.*

FAITH CLINIC-VOLUME VI-GRIEF CLINIC EDITION

Chapter 5

Stop With The Platitudes

SYMPTOM

🩺 OFFENDED BY OVERSIMPLIFICATION

You cringe at cliché responses like "They're in a better place" or "God makes no mistakes." These shallow phrases pierce deeper than comfort because they bypass your pain. You're left feeling unseen, invalidated, and spiritually dismissed.

If you've been grieving for longer than 48 hours, chances are somebody has said something to you that made you want to scream, *Please stop talking."* They meant well. They were trying to comfort you. But instead, what came out of their mouth was a platitude — a shallow, cookie-cutter phrase that sounded spiritual, but felt like salt in an open wound.

You've heard them. They usually come in the form of one-liners people grab when they don't know what else to say:

- *They're in a better place."*
- *God needed another angel."*
- *Everything happens for a reason."*
- *Time heals all wounds."*
- *At least they're not suffering anymore."*
- *You just need to be strong."*

Here's the problem: platitudes are easy for the speaker, but heavy for the grieving. They let the other person off the hook — they don't have to sit in your pain, they don't have to hold your silence, they don't have to risk saying the wrong thing if they just recycle a canned phrase. But for you, the one grieving? These words don't comfort. They cut. They feel dismissive. They shut down your pain instead of acknowledging it.

Let's break a few of them down.

They're in a better place." Okay, maybe that's true if they knew Christ. Heaven is real. Eternity is beautiful. But let's be brutally honest — the fact that they're in a better place doesn't change the fact that you're in a miserable one right now.

You don't get to hug them. You don't get to hear their voice. You don't get to share milestones. You don't get to sit across from them at the dinner table. Heaven may comfort theology, but it doesn't erase the ache of absence in your living room.

God needed another angel." First of all, theologically — that's wrong. Humans don't become angels. Angels are separate beings. And God doesn't "need" anything. He didn't take your loved one because He ran short on help in heaven. That phrase is not just unhelpful, it's unbiblical. And when you're grieving, the last thing you need is bad theology wrapped in a bow.

Everything happens for a reason." Maybe. But that reason might not comfort you right now, and most times the person saying it doesn't know the reason either. They just want to shut the conversation down. That phrase tells you, "Don't ask questions. Don't wrestle. Don't feel." It pretends to offer closure but blocks your process.

At least they're not suffering anymore." That might be true, but guess what? You are suffering. You're the one left behind. Your suffering doesn't vanish because theirs did. That line often feels like a dismissal of your pain.

And then the kicker: ***Be strong."*** People love to tell the grieving to be strong. Translation? "Please don't make us uncomfortable with your tears." But strength is not the absence of tears. Strength is showing up anyway. Strength is letting yourself feel. Strength is getting out of bed when your body doesn't want to.

The symptom here is clear: platitudes don't heal; they hurt. They create shame in the grieving heart. They make you wonder, *Am I doing this wrong? Should I be more spiritual, more strong, more thankful, less sad?"* Instead of letting you grieve, they rush you. Instead of validating your pain, they minimize it.

And here's the dark side: sometimes you start repeating these platitudes to yourself, because you've heard them so much. You catch yourself saying, "Everything happens for a reason" — even when it feels hollow. Or "They're in a better place" — even when you still ache for them here. You start parroting clichés as a survival mechanism, but they don't heal. They just cover your wounds with spiritual duct tape.

That's the symptom: you're surrounded by shallow comfort that doesn't actually comfort. People mean well, but their words make you feel *more* isolated, not less.

Platitudes aren't medicine. They're band-aids that don't stick. And they leave you with this haunting feeling: nobody wants to hear the truth of your pain.

FAITH CLINIC-VOLUME VI-GRIEF CLINIC EDITION

🧰 GRIEF CLINIC TOOLKIT 🧰

Tool For Oversimplification: Ecclesiastes 7:16

Here's the hard truth: platitudes aren't comfort — they're avoidance. They're what people say when they don't have the courage to sit with you in your pain. They're filler words. And while they may feel "safe" for the speaker, they often feel like daggers for the griever.

Platitudes fail for three reasons:

1. They minimize the pain.

Platitudes are shortcuts. Instead of saying, *I know this hurts so badly, and I don't know what to say, but I'm here,"* they give you a one-liner. *They're in a better place."* It's like trying to cover a gunshot wound with a band-aid. Sure, it sticks for a second, but it doesn't stop the bleeding. When you hear one, you feel like your grief is being shrunk down to something bite-sized and tidy, when the truth is your loss is massive, messy, and anything but tidy.

2. They put the burden back on you.

When someone says, *Be strong"* or *Time heals all wounds,"* what they're really saying is, "I don't want to deal with your pain, so please hurry up and deal with it yourself." Platitudes push responsibility back onto the grieving person, making you feel like you're failing if you're not "better" fast enough. Instead of comfort, you feel pressure. Instead of presence, you feel performance.

3. They misrepresent God.

This one stings the most. Some platitudes sound spiritual but completely butcher scripture. *God needed another angel"* is flat-out bad theology — humans don't become angels. *God won t give you more than you can handle"* is a misquoted verse (**1 Corinthians 10:13** is about temptation, not grief). And *Everything happens for a reason"* reduces a complex God to a cold chess master who moves people around like disposable pawns. These statements don't reflect God's heart — they distort it. And when you're already angry or confused with God, bad theology can wound your faith even more.

So, what does actual comfort look like? Let's look at Jesus.

When His friend Lazarus died, Jesus showed up to the funeral scene. Now, Jesus could have said a platitude. He could have told Mary and Martha, *Don t cry, he s in a better place."* Or, *Don t worry, everything happens for a reason."* Or, *Time heals all wounds."* But He didn't. Instead, **John 11:35** records the shortest — and maybe most important — verse in the Bible: **"Jesus wept."**

That s what real comfort looks like: not words, but presence, and free flowing emotions. Not pat answers, but shared tears. Jesus didn't minimize the pain by saying "Don't worry, resurrection is coming." He entered the pain. He wept in it.

The Bible shows us repeatedly that comfort is not about fixing; it's about being. In **Job 2:13**, when Job's friends first arrived, they did the right thing: *They sat on the ground with him for seven days and seven nights. No one said a word to him, because they saw how great his suffering was."* Before they opened their mouths and ruined everything with bad theology, they were good friends. Why? Because they sat in silence. They didn't rush. They didn't explain. They just existed with him.

FAITH CLINIC-VOLUME VI-GRIEF CLINIC EDITION

That's what grieving people need. Not empty phrases, but presence. Not rushed closure, but space. Not theological shortcuts, but the kind of love that says, *I don t know what to say, but I m not leaving.*"

Tool For Your Kit: words can wound, but presence can heal.

It doesn't mean words are useless. Scripture says, *A word in season, how good it is!"* (**Proverbs 15:23**). The right words matter — but the right words are honest, compassionate, and humble.

They sound more like:

- *I don t have the right words, but I m here."*

- *This is unfair, and I m so sorry."*

- *You don t have to be strong with me."*

- *Tell me about them. I d love to hear a memory."*

See the difference? Those words don't try to fix. They make room. They acknowledge the weight of the loss instead of rushing you out of it.

And here s where faith comes in: God doesn't deal in platitudes either. He doesn't look at your broken heart and say, *Everything happens for a reason."* No — He says, *The Lord is close to the brokenhearted and saves those who are crushed in spirit"* (**Psalm 34:18**).

He doesn't say, *Be strong."* He says, *My grace is sufficient for you, for My power is made perfect in weakness"* (**2 Corinthians 12:9**). He doesn't tell you, *Time heals all wounds."* He says, *I heal the brokenhearted and bind up their wounds"* (**Psalm 147:3**).

God's comfort is not cliché — it's concrete. It's His presence, His Spirit, His Word. And unlike people's empty phrases, His words have weight. They hold. They anchor. They breathe life back into places that feel dead.

Here's the tool: platitudes fail because they're shallow, but God's comfort works because it's real. He doesn't ask you to fake it. He doesn't shame you for weeping. He doesn't minimize your pain. He sits with you in it. He wept at a tomb. He sweat drops of blood in Gethsemane. He knows grief. And because He knows it, He knows how to comfort it.

You don't need clichés. You need Christ.

SPIRITUAL VITAMIN

Daily Dose: *Platitudes may hush people, but God's comfort heals hearts."*

Here's your vitamin — chewable, repeatable, necessary every morning. Platitudes are designed to keep things tidy for everyone else. They hush the awkwardness, silence the tension, and let people feel like they, "said something." But they don't heal you. In fact, sometimes they make you feel more alone.

God's comfort, however, doesn't hush you — it heals you. He doesn't silence your sobs; He sits with them. He doesn't rush you to closure; He walks with you through chaos. He doesn't try to explain away your pain; He enters it. That's the difference between platitudes and presence. One quiets *others*. The other restores *you*.

So, every day, take this vitamin: remind yourself that comfort isn't about who texted you or what people said at the funeral. It's about the Spirit of God who still whispers, *I am with you always."*

HOLY SPIRIT CONSULT

Picture this: you're sitting in the Faith Clinic exam chair, rolling your eyes at the last "comfort" someone gave you. The Holy Spirit leans forward and says:

You don't need their phrases. You need My presence."

That's the consultation.

People will say things that sting. Some of them will even mean well. But their words aren't the authority on your grief. The Spirit is. He is the Counselor (**John 14:26**). That's literally His job description — to remind you of God's truth when the world offers cheap substitutes.

The Spirit whispers: *I will never throw you clichés. I will tell you truth. I don't hush your pain. I heal it. Let Me retrain your ears to recognize My voice above theirs."*

The consultation is simple: stop feeding on platitudes. Start listening for Presence. Because the Spirit doesn't do soundbites — He does soul care.

Guided Prayer + Declarations

Prayer
"*God, I admit that people's words have sometimes cut deeper than they comforted. I know they meant well, but clichés don't heal my heart — Your presence does.*

Thank You that You are the God of all comfort, not the God of empty phrases. Teach me to run to You when words feel hollow. Remind me that You sit with me, cry with me, and speak truth when others don't know what to say. Help me to forgive people who said the wrong things and help me to listen for Your voice above the noise of theirs. Amen."

Declarations (say these out loud until they stick):

- I declare that I don't need clichés — I need Christ.

- I declare that God's comfort is stronger than people's empty words.

- I declare that presence is greater than platitudes.

- I declare that God's Word heals me more deeply than any one-liner.

- I declare that my grief does not need to be rushed or silenced to make others comfortable.

Journal + Reflection Page

Take some time with these prompts — honesty is the treatment here:

4. **What is the most frustrating or hurtful "platitude" someone has said to you in your grief?** How did it make you feel?

_____
_____
_____
_____
_____

FAITH CLINIC-VOLUME VI-GRIEF CLINIC EDITION

5. **Why do you think people default to clichés instead of honesty when faced with grief?** What does that say about their own discomfort with pain?

6. **Read 2 Corinthians 1:3–4 again slowly.** Write down how God has comforted you personally so far in your grief journey.

7. If you could rewrite one of the common clichés (*They re in a better place,"* *"Be strong,"* *"Time heals"*) into a phrase that actually comforts, what would you say instead?

   _____
   _____
   _____
   _____
   _____
   _____
   _____

8. Write a short prayer giving your grief back to God, asking Him to replace the noise of people's words with the truth of His Word.

   _____
   _____
   _____
   _____
   _____

 Closing Note

Platitudes may silence awkward moments, but they don't soothe shattered hearts. People's phrases will fail, but God's presence never does. You don't need to swallow clichés like medicine — you need to let the Comforter Himself sit with you in the ache.

Here s the takeaway: when you hear the next shallow phrase tossed your way, don't let it sink into your spirit. Let it roll off and run straight back to the God who doesn't hand out one-liners but wraps you in real comfort. Because grief doesn't need platitudes. It needs presence. And you already have His.

"Pain doesn't need a proverb—it needs presence. When hearts are broken, don't offer clichés. Offer comfort."

-DR. PATRICIA S. TANNER

FAITH CLINIC-VOLUME VI-GRIEF CLINIC EDITION

Chapter 6

When Grief Hits The Body Too

DR. PATRICIA S. TANNER

SYMPTOM

PHYSICAL MANIFESTATIONS OF EMOTIONAL PAIN

Grief begins to show up in your body—fatigue, headaches, chest tightness, insomnia, or digestive issues. The weight of loss settles not just in your spirit, but in your physical frame, making even daily tasks feel like a burden.

Nobody warns you how much grief will wreck your body. People expect tears, maybe mood swings, even anger. But nobody prepares you for the physical toll. Grief is not just something you *feel* in your heart — it's something you *carry* in your body. And carrying loss is exhausting.

Let's talk about fatigue first. Grief is bone-deep tiredness. It's not the kind of tired a nap can fix. It's waking up already exhausted, like your body is dragging an invisible weight all day long. Sleep doesn't restore you, because grief keeps you restless. Nights are filled with tossing, turning, or waking up at 2 a.m. remembering they're gone. And mornings? They feel like mountains you don't want to climb.

Then there's the infamous "grief brain." Forgetfulness. Foggy thinking. Losing your keys three times in one day. Standing in a room with no idea why you walked in there. Reading the same sentence repeatedly but not absorbing a word. It's like your brain is on strike. And honestly? It is. Your mind is so consumed with loss that it has fewer resources to handle everyday tasks. That's why grieving people often feel like they're "losing it." But you're not losing your mind — your mind is just overloaded.

And let's not forget the body aches. Grief literally hurts. Your chest feels tight. Your shoulders stay tense. Your stomach knots. You might even feel phantom pains, because your body is expressing what your spirit can't put into words. Science backs this up — stress hormones flood your body when you're grieving, which weakens your immune system, messes with your appetite, and makes you prone to sickness. Ever notice how many people catch colds, flare up old conditions, or develop new health issues after a major loss? That's grief's calling card.

Here s the kicker: society rarely acknowledges grief's physical impact. People expect you to bounce back into your normal routines — work, family, church, responsibilities — like your body isn't dragging itself through quicksand. They don't realize that even simple tasks like grocery shopping or folding laundry can feel Olympic level. They don't understand that "just getting out of bed" is sometimes the greatest act of bravery you can offer.

And so, you start feeling guilty. You think, *Why can t I function? Why am I so tired? Why can t I focus?"* You blame yourself for being "lazy" or "weak," when your body is simply telling the truth about your grief. It's responding to trauma. It's showing you — in the form of fatigue, fog, and aches — that loss isn't just emotional. It's holistic. It hits every part of you.

The symptom is this: grief doesn't just break your heart; it breaks into your body. It hijacks your energy, steals your focus, and leaves you feeling physically drained. And when people around you don't understand that you carry not only the weight of grief but also the shame of feeling like you're "failing" at everyday life.

And let's be brutally honest — this is where platitudes and "get back to normal" pressures hit hardest. When you're exhausted from simply existing, people start dropping comments like, *You just need to push through"* or *Get back into your routine."* But routines don't cure grief brain. Pushing through doesn't erase exhaustion. If anything, it makes you more drained.

Your body knows the truth your soul can't hide: grief is work. It's not passive. It demands energy, attention, and effort. And just like physical labor, it wears you out. That's why you're tired, achy, and foggy. Not because you're broken — because you're grieving.

Here s the symptom: grief is not just emotional chaos. It's physical. It's exhausting. It takes over your body, and if you don't acknowledge that, you'll spend your days wondering why you can't "just get it together."

GRIEF CLINIC TOOLKIT

Tool For Physical Grief Manifestations: Matthew 11:28

When your body feels like it's collapsing under the weight of grief, the last thing you need is someone telling you to "just keep going." Yet that's the soundtrack many of us hear from culture, family, and sometimes even the church: *Stay strong." Keep pushing." Don t let it get to you."* But let's tell the truth — grief already got to you. It got to your body, your mind, your sleep, your focus, and your strength. Pretending otherwise doesn't make you holy, it just makes you tired.

The beauty of scripture is that God doesn't shame human weakness. He names it. He sees it. And He steps right into it.

Take Elijah in **1 Kings 19**. This man had just faced down prophets of Baal, prayed fire from heaven, and seen God show up in miraculous power. But right after the mountaintop victory came collapse.

He ran into the wilderness, sat under a tree, and begged God to take his life. That's not just emotional exhaustion — that's physical and spiritual burnout colliding. And what did God do? Did He lecture Elijah? Tell him to "man up" or "pray harder"? No. God sent an angel who told him to *eat and rest*. Twice. Because God knew that exhaustion needs nourishment, not condemnation.

For Your Toolkit: God validates grief wearing your body down. He knows you can't think straight when you're running on fumes. He knows your immune system can't heal when your spirit is crushed. He knows the body isn't an accessory to grief — it's a participant. And His prescription is not "try harder" but "rest deeper."

Think about Jesus in the Garden of Gethsemane. **Luke 22:44** describes Him as being in *anguish"* so intense that His sweat was like drops of blood. That's not symbolic poetry — that's physical manifestation of deep grief. His body literally responded to the spiritual weight He was carrying. And when He turned to His closest friends for support, they fell asleep. He didn't have cheerleaders telling Him He was "so strong." He had a body shaking under the strain of grief. And He still carried it to the cross.

If Jesus Himself experienced grief so heavy it showed up in His body, why would we think we're exempt? Why would we think we should just "bounce back" when the Savior Himself groaned under the weight of sorrow?

This is why guilt has no place in your healing process. If you're tired, achy, or foggy, it's not a sign that you're failing. It's a sign that you're human. And being human is not a sin. It's the design. Even the psalmist cries out in **Psalm 31:9-10**:

Be merciful to me, LORD, for I am in distress; my eyes grow weak with sorrow, my soul and body with grief. My life is consumed by anguish and my years by groaning; my strength fails because of my affliction, and my bones grow weak."

That verse doesn't hide the physical effects of grief. It puts them front and center. Weak eyes. Failing strength. Weak bones. Scripture literally validates what you're experiencing right now.

And yet — here's the hope: God never leaves the body to fend for itself. He is the God who restores strength. **Isaiah 40:29** says: *He gives strength to the weary and increases the power of the weak."* Not the strong. Not the ones who pretend they're fine. The weary. The weak. That's who He meets with fresh power.

See, the world tells you to "power through." God tells you to *lean in*. The world says, "fake strength." God says, "come to me, all who are weary and burdened, and I will give you rest" (**Matthew 11:28**). Rest is not laziness. Rest is obedience. Rest is faith in action.

Grief whispers, *You'll never feel normal again."* God whispers, *Even youths grow tired and weary, but those who hope in the Lord will renew their strength. They will soar on wings like eagles; they will run and not grow weary; they will walk and not faint"* (**Isaiah 40:30-31**). Notice the order: soar, run, walk. Sometimes grief won't let you soar. Sometimes it won't even let you run. But walking — step by step, breath by breath — is still faith. And God calls even that holy.

The teaching here is simple but life-altering:

- Grief will hit your body, but God will meet you there.

- You don't have to explain your fatigue to Him. He already knows.

- Rest is not quitting — it's trusting.

- Weakness is not failure — it's the very place God pours out strength.

So, stop shaming yourself for being exhausted. Stop apologizing for brain fog. Stop pretending your body isn't screaming at you. Instead, listen to it. Honor it. Bring it to the One who designed it.

You don't heal by denying the symptoms. You heal by letting God step into the symptom with you. And if He prescribed rest for Elijah, and He carried the grief of Jesus through blood-sweating anguish, He will carry you too.

Because grief does hit the body, but so does resurrection power.

FAITH PRESCRIPTION

Think of this as the spiritual medicine the Great Physician writes out for you. No sugar coating, no generic brand substitutes—just the Word of God that goes straight to the core of your fatigue and weakness.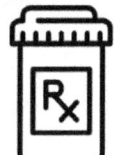
When grief hits your body, these prescriptions aren't just verses to glance at. They're truth to *take daily,* like life-saving medication for your soul.

- **Psalm 73:26** – *My flesh and my heart may fail, but God is the strength of my heart and my portion forever."*

    → <u>**Translation**</u>: Yes, your body feels like it's giving up. Yes, your heart feels like it's breaking. But God is not checking out when your strength runs out. He becomes your strength.

- **Isaiah 40:29** – *He gives strength to the weary and increases the power of the weak."*

→ **Translation**: He doesn't wait until you're "better" to help you. He meets you in the exact moment of your collapse.

- **Psalm 31:9-10** – *Be merciful to me, LORD, for I am in distress; my eyes grow weak with sorrow, my soul and body with grief."*

  → **Translation**: Scripture already validates what you feel: grief makes the body weak. You're not making it up. You're not exaggerating. This is real, and God sees it.

- **Matthew 11:28-30** – *Come to me, all you who are weary and burdened, and I will give you rest."*

  → **Translation**: Not another chore list. Not another religious hoop to jump through. Rest. God prescribes rest when your body is weighed down.

- **2 Corinthians 12:9** – *My grace is sufficient for you, for my power is made perfect in weakness."*

  → **Translation**: Your weakness is not disqualifying you. It's *qualifying* you for His strength.

💊 SPIRITUAL VITAMIN

Every Faith Clinic book includes a spiritual vitamin because grief, like sickness, depletes your reserves. You need something daily to rebuild what's been drained. For this chapter, the vitamin is:

💊 Vitamin R — REST in God's Presence

Take REST daily (or hourly, depending on the meltdown).

Rest isn't just about sleeping (though naps can be holy). Rest is about positioning your body and mind in the presence of God where striving stops. When you swallow this vitamin, you're reminding yourself:

- Rest is not weakness. It's worship.

- Rest doesn't mean giving up. It means giving *in* to God's care.

- Rest is the soil where healing grows.

Practical ways to take this vitamin:

- Schedule a Sabbath—even half a day where you stop performing and let yourself breathe.

- Set aside 10 minutes to sit in silence before God, no agenda. Just let Him hold you.

- Repeat **Matthew 11:28** out loud before bed: *Come to me, all you who are weary and burdened, and I will give you rest."*

Think of this as a supplement for your soul that tells your body: *You don't have to carry this alone.*

HOLY SPIRIT CONSULT

Now let's be real: in the *Faith Clinic*, the Holy Spirit is the attending physician. He doesn't just hand you a pamphlet and walk out of the room. He leans close, listens to the groans you don't have words for, and prescribes treatment tailored to *you*.

What the Holy Spirit might whisper in this chapter of your grief:

- *It s okay to lie down. Even Jesus rested in a boat during the storm."*

- *You don t need to explain why you re tired. I already know."*

- *Stop thinking rest means laziness. Rest is an act of trust."*

- *You are not being unspiritual when you admit you re exhausted. You re being honest—and I can work with honesty."*

The Holy Spirit doesn't shame your weakness; He supplies strength in the middle of it. **Romans 8:26** says: *The Spirit helps us in our weakness. We do not know what we ought to pray for, but the Spirit himself intercedes for us with groans too deep for words."*

That s the consult: the Spirit Himself is praying for you when you're too tired to lift your head. He is your advocate when grief steals your breath.

🙏 Guided Prayer + Declarations

Grief leaves you too exhausted to even form sentences sometimes, so here's a prayer you can lean on when your words feel broken.

Prayer:
"Lord, my body is tired. My chest feels heavy, my bones ache, and I don t even have the energy to explain it. You know how grief has drained me, how sorrow has pressed on my body like a weight I can t lift.

Today I bring this weakness to You. Be the strength I don t have. Teach me how to rest without shame, how to breathe without panic, and how to lean into Your presence when I m worn out. Let Your Spirit carry me when I cannot carry myself. Thank You that You don t despise my weakness but meet me in it. Amen."

Declarations: (Speak these over yourself, even when you don't feel them. Truth works even when you're numb.)

1. My weakness is not my failure; it's my place of God's strength.

2. I give myself permission to rest, because God has already granted it.

3. My body is not betraying me—it is signaling my need for His care.

4. The Spirit intercedes for me when I have no words.

5. Jesus Himself invites me into rest; I will not resist His invitation.

📄 Journal + Reflection Page

Reflection Prompts :

- **Where in your body do you feel grief the most (headaches, stomach, back, fatigue)?** Write it down.

_____
_____
_____
_____
_____
_____
_____

- How have you judged yourself for being "weak" when you were just grieving?

- What lies have you believed about rest (for example: "rest = laziness")? Replace them with truths from scripture.

- **What does "rest in God's presence" look like for you in this season—practical, not lofty (a nap, a slow walk, quiet time in prayer)?**

📓 Journal Space:

Use this page to unload the heaviness. Write a letter to your body as if it were your closest friend:

- Thank it for carrying you through grief, even when it feels broken.

- Acknowledge where it hurts.

- Speak kindness over it. (Example: "Dear Body, I know you're tired. You're not weak for needing rest. I love you, and I give you permission to heal.")

DR. PATRICIA S. TANNER

Sometimes healing starts with how you speak to yourself.

FAITH CLINIC-VOLUME VI-GRIEF CLINIC EDITION

Chapter 7

Faith Feels Flat-Worship Songs Sound Like Elevator Music

DR. PATRICIA S. TANNER

SYMPTOM

❦ NUMBNESS TOWARDS SPIRITUAL PRACTICES

You no longer "feel" God during worship, prayer, or reading the Word. Faith feels distant and disconnected—like you're mouthing words to songs your heart can't sing. Grief has muffled your spirit, and once-powerful encounters with God now seem dull and unresponsive.

There's a moment in grief when faith doesn't "feel" like faith anymore. Worship songs that once had you raising your hands now sound like background noise in a lobby you're just passing through. The lyrics don't hit, the prayers don't stir, and opening your Bible feels about as thrilling as reading the back of a shampoo bottle.

It's not that you've stopped believing in God — it's that your emotions checked out. Numbness creeps in. And numbness is terrifying, because at least when you're crying, you feel alive. At least when you're angry, you feel something. But numb? Numb is silence. Numb is absence. Numb is floating through church services wondering if you're just a fraud in a pew.

Grief brings this numbness like an unwanted roommate. You're not trying to be unspiritual. You're not rejecting God. You're just…empty. And emptiness is exhausting, because everyone around you expects passion, fire, revival energy — while you're just trying not to yawn through the chorus of the same worship song played for the 147th Sunday in a row.

FAITH CLINIC-VOLUME VI-GRIEF CLINIC EDITION

The symptom here is clear: grief drains the color out of your spiritual life, and suddenly everything feels muted. You don't feel God the way you used to, and you wonder if that means He's gone.

There's a very particular stage of grief that no one warns you about. People will tell you about the tears, the anger, the bargaining, the questions, even the denial. But very few mention the numbness — the heavy, blank space that comes when your emotions simply tap out. At first, grief feels like a storm — loud, uncontrollable, overwhelming. But eventually, the storm shifts, and instead of thunder, you're left with silence. Not peace-filled silence, but hollow silence. That's where spiritual numbness often shows up.

For many grieving hearts, this numbness bleeds into their relationship with God. Songs that used to stir tears now sound like elevator background noise. The first few chords of a once-beloved worship song now feel routine, maybe even annoying. Lyrics you once clung to now pass over you like air-conditioning — you notice it faintly, but you don't feel moved.

You sit in church and wonder why everyone else seems "caught up" in a moment of glory while you're fighting sleep, boredom, or irritation. You think: *What's wrong with me? Have I lost faith? Have I somehow offended God by not "feeling" Him anymore?*

This is the symptom: a flat, disconnected spiritual life where grief numbs your ability to feel. It's not that you've stopped believing in God, but it feels like your soul has stopped responding to Him.

And it doesn't only happen in church. Prayer, too, becomes flat. You kneel, fold your hands, or close your eyes, but the words feel mechanical. Where once you could pour out your heart in tears, now you mutter short sentences, unsure if they even matter. Opening the Bible feels daunting — where do you even start when your heart feels shut down? Scriptures that used to leap off the page now feel like words in a foreign language you're too tired to translate.

The numbness feels like betrayal. Because if you've grown up in church, you've been conditioned to believe that *feeling* God's presence is a measure of your spiritual health. That the goosebumps, the tears, the fire in your chest during worship are signs of God's closeness. And so, when grief numbs those feelings, you begin to doubt yourself: *Am I even saved? Did I lose the Holy Spirit? Am I faithless now?*

This symptom is not just about apathy — it's about guilt stacked on top of grief. Because while you're already battling the pain of loss, you're now carrying the shame of not "*feeling*" spiritual.

Here's the raw truth: numbness in grief is not rebellion. It's not evidence that you've abandoned God. It's evidence that your body, mind, and spirit are overloaded. Numbness is the nervous system's survival strategy. When grief hits, your brain can only process so much. So, it shuts down excess emotional responses to protect you. That includes the emotional highs of worship.

Think about it this way: when you're physically sick and your body shuts down appetite, it's not because food stopped being good — it's because your system is too overwhelmed to process it. Spiritual numbness works the same way. God didn't stop being good. Worship didn't stop being powerful. Scripture didn't stop being alive. Your soul is just temporarily too overloaded to *feel* it all.

But because no one preaches about numbness, you think you're broken. You look at others swaying in worship, tears falling down their cheeks, hands lifted high, and you feel like an imposter. Like you're sitting in the wrong room. Like you've somehow disqualified yourself from intimacy with God.

This is why we need to diagnose this symptom for what it is: spiritual numbness in grief is real, but it does not equal spiritual death. It's the body's way of cushioning an already shattered heart. It's the spirit's way of saying, *"I'm still here, but I need time."*

And naming it matters, because until you call it what it is, you'll keep misdiagnosing yourself. You'll confuse numbness with backsliding. You'll confuse survival mode with faithlessness. You'll confuse temporary silence with permanent absence.

Here's the first dose of truth: if worship songs sound like elevator music right now, you're not faithless — you're grieving. If prayer feels empty, you're not broken — you're in survival mode. And if scripture feels dull, you're not abandoned — you're simply overloaded.

This numbness is not proof that God left you.
It's proof that your soul is human. And even numb souls are still held by God's hands.

Faith Without Feelings Is Still Faith

Now let's flip the light on. If numbness is the symptom, what's the truth that steadies us? It's this: faith has never been about feelings. Feelings may *accompany* faith, but they are not the foundation of it.

The Bible never equates goosebumps with belief. It never says that tears during worship equal intimacy with God. It never says that passion, energy, or spiritual fireworks are the measure of your standing before Him. In fact, scripture goes out of its way to say the opposite.

Romans 1:17 tells us: *"The righteous shall live by faith."* Not by feelings. Not by emotional highs. By faith.

Faith is an anchor, not a vibe. And anchors are especially crucial when the waves of grief are tossing you.

Let's take Job for example. Job wasn't singing "Way maker" with hands raised when his life fell apart. He was sitting in ashes, scraping his wounds, barely able to breathe. And yet his words echo through history: *"Though he slay me, yet will I hope in Him"* (**Job 13:15**). That's not emotional worship — that's raw survival trust. That's faith when all feelings are dead.

Or consider Jesus on the cross. In the most pivotal moment of history, He cried out, *"My God, my God, why have you forsaken me?"* (**Matthew 27:46**). That's not a feeling of closeness. That's the Son of God Himself admitting that He *felt* abandoned. Yet even in that numb, forsaken cry, He was still fulfilling the Father's will. Still obedient. Still faithful.

Faith, then, is not what you feel in the moment. Faith is what you cling to even when you feel nothing.

Now, let's get practical. Many believers wrestle with guilt because their grief makes worship feel fake. They think: *If I don't feel anything when I sing, am I lying to God?* The truth? No. Singing when you don't feel it is not lying — it's obedience. And obedience is the deepest form of worship.

Anyone can sing when the feelings flow. But lifting your voice in numbness is like planting seeds in a drought — it looks pointless, but it proves you believe rain will come again.

That's why Hebrews 11 is called the "Hall of Faith" and not the "Hall of Feelings." Abraham didn't feel like leaving everything familiar. Noah didn't feel like building an ark for decades with zero rain in sight. Moses didn't feel like leading whiny people through the wilderness. But faith isn't about feelings — it's about obedience when feelings are absent.

This teaching dismantles one of grief's biggest lies: *"If I can't feel God, I must not have faith."* Wrong. Real faith is built precisely when you don't feel Him and still show up.

- ✓ If worship feels flat, but you still whisper the lyrics — that's faith.

- ✓ If prayer feels like static, but you still say, "God, I'm here" — that's faith.

- ✓ If scripture feels dry, but you still open the book — that's faith.

Faith without feelings is still faith. In fact, it might be stronger faith, because it's stripped of emotional props. It's just raw, stubborn trust. And that's the kind of faith God honors.

Here's the final shift: stop panicking when you don't feel God. The absence of feelings is not the absence of His presence. He's just as close in silence as He is in the shout.

So let yourself rest. Stop waiting for goosebumps to prove God loves you. Stop treating numbness like failure. Keep showing up. That's the deepest worship you can give in grief.

GRIEF CLINIC TOOLKIT

<u>**Tool To Release Numbness**</u>: Romans 1:17

Here's the shocker: your feelings were never the measure of your faith in the first place. The Bible never said, "The righteous shall live by goosebumps." It says, *The righteous will live by faith"* **(Romans 1:17).**

That means when worship feels flat, God is still worthy. When prayer feels like talking to drywall, He's still listening. When scripture feels like words on a page instead of fire in your chest, it's still alive and active.

Think about Job. This man lost everything — children, wealth, health — and what does he do? He sits in ashes, barely able to breathe, and says, *Though he slay me, yet will I hope in him"* **(Job 13:15).** That wasn't faith that felt good.

That was faith stripped of feelings. That was raw, ugly, un-pretty trust. Faith isn't the high of worship. It isn't the tears that fall when a song matches your mood. Faith is waking up and whispering, "I'm still here, God," even when you don't feel Him.

And let's be clear: numbness doesn't disqualify you. Jesus didn't say, "Blessed are the ones who feel me." He said, *Blessed are those who have not seen and yet have believed"* **(John 20:29).** That includes those who don't always feel Him but still show up.

Here's the bottom line: God doesn't grade your faith on emotions. He honors your faith when you show up in silence, when you choose Him in the numbness, when you keep holding on even when your soul feels flatlined.

FAITH CLINIC-VOLUME VI-GRIEF CLINIC EDITION

FAITH PRESCRIPTION

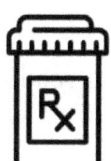
Let's be real: when grief makes faith feel flat, the last thing you want to do is "show up." Showing up feels like work. You don't want to sing when it feels fake. You don't want to pray when it feels empty. You don't want to read the Bible when your eyes glaze over after two verses. And yet, here's the paradox of healing: showing up is exactly what keeps you alive spiritually — even when you feel nothing while doing it.

Think of it like physical rehab after an injury. When a person breaks a leg, the doctors don't say, "Well, since walking is painful right now, just stay in bed forever." No. They prescribe physical therapy. At first, therapy feels pointless. The muscles are weak. The pain is sharp. Progress feels invisible. But if the person keeps showing up, one day they notice strength returning. Numbness fades. The body remembers what it was made to do.

Faith in grief works the same way. Spiritual numbness doesn't mean you stop moving. It means you move by choice, not by feelings. You keep walking into worship, prayer, and scripture, not because they feel good, but because they *are* good.

This is where the power of discipline shows up. Discipline is a dirty word in some church circles, because we'd rather be swept away by emotion than tethered by routine. But discipline is what holds you when feelings fail you. It's what ties your soul to God when grief cuts all other ropes.

Showing up doesn't mean faking it. It doesn't mean plastering on a smile during worship or forcing yourself to raise your hands when your arms feel like lead. It means bringing your numb self into God's presence anyway. Even if all you can do is sit quietly. Even if all you can whisper is, *"Lord, I'm here."*

Here's the key: consistency beats intensity. If you can only manage five minutes of prayer, give those five minutes every day. If you can only read one verse without zoning out, then read that verse every day. Don't despise the small doses.

God doesn't grade your faith by how many chapters you read or how loud you sang. He delights in your presence, even if all you brought was your broken, silent self.

The prescription is simple, but not easy: ***show up anyway***.

- Show up to church, even if the music feels like background noise.

- Show up to prayer, even if your words feel weak.

- Show up to scripture, even if your eyes skim more than they absorb.

- Show up to God, even if you can only sit in silence.

Why? Because healing isn't in the feeling. Healing is in the showing up.

Psalm 34:18 says: *"The Lord is close to the brokenhearted and saves those who are crushed in spirit."* Notice it doesn't say "The Lord feels close." It says He *is* close. Whether you feel Him or not, He's there. And the act of showing up is how you train your spirit to believe that truth, even when emotions haven't caught up yet.

Think of Thomas, the disciple. After Jesus' death, Thomas was so numb and skeptical that he said he wouldn't believe unless he touched Jesus' wounds. But here's the detail we often miss: even in his doubt, Thomas still showed up. **John 20** tells us that Thomas was with the other disciples when Jesus appeared. He could have isolated himself in his grief. He could have disappeared into silence. But he stayed in the room. And because he stayed, he saw Jesus.

That's the prescription for you, too: don't disappear. Stay in the room. Keep showing up. Even if you don't feel it, even if you don't believe much right now, even if your numbness tells you, it's pointless. Because one day — maybe not today, maybe not tomorrow — Jesus will walk into the room, and you'll see Him again.

Take these verses daily (out loud if possible):

- **Hebrews 11:1** — *Now faith is confidence in what we hope for and assurance about what we do not see."*

- **Psalm 73:26** — *My flesh and my heart may fail, but God is the strength of my heart and my portion forever."*

- **Isaiah 40:31** — *But those who hope in the Lord will renew their strength. They will soar on wings like eagles; they will run and not grow weary; they will walk and not be faint."*

Repeat until your spirit remembers that faith isn't about how you feel — it's about who God is.

💊 SPIRITUAL VITAMIN

Vitamin F (Faith Over Feelings)

Take as often as needed. This supplement reminds your soul that numbness doesn't mean abandonment. The active ingredient is God's unchanging presence, which does not expire when your emotions do. Side effects include unexpected strength, quiet resilience, and the ability to worship without waiting on your feelings to catch up.

Every prescription needs a daily supplement — a spiritual vitamin that nourishes you from the inside out. For this chapter, the vitamin is **Romans 8:26:**

"In the same way, the Spirit helps us in our weakness. We do not know what we ought to pray for, but the Spirit Himself intercedes for us through wordless groans."

This verse is a lifeline for the spiritually numb. It means that when your prayers feel empty, you're not praying alone. When you sit in silence, God isn't judging you — His Spirit is praying for you.

Think about that: the Holy Spirit is not just near you; He's literally filling the gap between your numb heart and God's throne. He takes your sighs, your groans, your silence, and translates them into intercession. When you mutter, "God, I don't even know what to say," the Spirit whispers, *"I've got this."*

That's why this verse is your vitamin. Because vitamins don't always make you feel different immediately. You don't swallow a capsule and feel energy in two minutes. No — vitamins nourish you slowly, building your strength day after day until one day you realize your body is stronger, steadier, and healthier.

Romans 8:26 is like that. You may not "feel" the Spirit interceding. But He is. Every groan, every tear, every silent prayer becomes fuel for your healing because the Spirit is carrying it to the Father.

Here's your daily dose: when you don't know what to pray, sit still and breathe. Whisper this scripture: *"The Spirit helps me in my weakness."* Repeat it until it sinks in. You don't need eloquent words. You don't need emotional fire. You just need to trust that the Spirit is speaking on your behalf.

And when you sing worship songs that feel like elevator music? Remember — the Spirit is harmonizing with you. Even if your voice feels flat, His intercession is rich.

HOLY SPIRIT CONSULT

Picture the Holy Spirit as the gentle counselor sitting next to you in the silence. He doesn't rush you. He doesn't shame you. He simply stays. **Romans 8:26** says the Spirit intercedes for us with groans too deep for words. That means when worship songs feel like elevator music, the Spirit Himself is singing for you. When your prayers feel like static, He's translating them. When you're numb, He's not.

The consultation is simple: stop panicking about what you can't feel. The Spirit is working underneath it all.

Now let's picture this through the Faith Clinic lens: you've got a prescription (show up anyway) and a vitamin (**Romans 8:26**). But what about your consult with the Specialist — the Holy Spirit Himself?

Jesus called the Spirit our **Comforter (John 14:26)**. Notice the timing: comfort is not needed when life feels great. Comfort is needed when pain numbs you. The Spirit is not offended by your silence. He's not put off by your lack of tears in worship. He doesn't storm out of the room when you zone out during prayer. He sits with you.

One of the most powerful truths about the Spirit is this: He is a Presence, not a performance. His role is not to make you "feel spiritual" but to remind you that you are never abandoned. Even in the flat, numb, empty seasons, He is whispering truth to your soul.

Here's what the Holy Spirit might say in your consult:

- *"Stop worrying about feelings. I am here, even in your silence."*

- *"You are not faithless just because you are numb."*

- *"I am translating your sighs into prayers. Nothing is wasted."*

- *"Your showing up matters more than your emotions right now."*

The Spirit's comfort often looks like presence without words. Like a friend who sits with you in the hospital waiting room, not filling the air with clichés, but simply refusing to leave your side. That's the Spirit in your numbness. He doesn't need you to perform. He just needs you to breathe, and He'll do the rest.

 Guided Prayer + Declarations

Prayer:
"God, I feel nothing right now, and that scares me. I don't want to confuse numbness with unbelief. Help me to trust You even when my emotions are shut down. Thank You that Your love doesn't depend on how I feel but on who You are. Teach me to keep showing up, even when it feels flat. Let my faith hold steady in the silence, knowing that You are still speaking, even if my heart is slow to hear.

Father, I come before You today with honesty. My worship feels flat. My prayers feel dry. My heart feels numb. And yet, here I am. I'm showing up, not because I feel strong, but because I need You more than ever. Lord, remind me that faith is not about my emotions — it's about my trust in You. Even when I can't sense You, teach me to believe that You are near. Even when the songs feel empty, let my presence in Your presence be my offering.

Holy Spirit, help me rest in the truth that You intercede for me when I don't have the words. Translate my sighs, my silence, and my tears into prayers that reach the Father's heart. Keep me from walking away when faith feels pointless. Give me endurance to keep showing up, even if all I can do is sit quietly before You. Remind me that Your love is not measured by my feelings, but by Your faithfulness.

Jesus, You know grief. You know numbness. You know silence. You wept, You groaned, and You endured. Sit with me in this numb place and let me borrow Your strength until mine returns. I don't ask for hype or feelings — I ask for You. Be near, even when I can't perceive You. Amen."

Declarations:

Speak these out loud when your emotions don't line up with truth. Remember — your faith builds by what you declare.

1. I declare that faith is not a feeling — it is trust in God's character.

2. I declare that my numbness does not mean God has left me. He is still here.

3. I declare that showing up matters more than how I feel when I show up.

4. I declare that the Holy Spirit prays for me when I cannot pray for myself.

5. I declare that silence is not failure — it is space for God's comfort.

6. I declare that one day my numbness will be lifted, but until then, I will remain in His presence.

7. I declare that I am not faithless — I am faithful in the way I continue to show up.

8. I declare that Jesus is with me in every worship song, every quiet prayer, and every flat season.

9. I declare that healing will come not by my striving, but by God's steady grace.

10. I declare that my grief is not the end of my story — God is still writing my worship.

📝 Journal + Reflection Page

Take 15–20 minutes to sit with these prompts. Don't force "deep" answers. Even one word or sentence matters. This is your faith showing up on paper.

1. **When was the last time worship or prayer felt flat to you?** Write it down honestly.

_____
_____
_____
_____
_____
_____
_____
_____
_____
_____

2. **What lie tries to attach itself to your numbness?** (Example: "God must not love me," or "I must not have real faith.")

3. **Write a truth from scripture that you can use to replace that lie. (Romans 8:26** is a good place to start.)

4. **How can you "show up" this week, even if it's in a small way?** (Ex: reading one verse daily, whispering one prayer, sitting in silence for five minutes.)

_____
_____
_____
_____
_____
_____
_____
_____

5. **What would you say to a friend who told you they felt numb in their faith?** Write it as if you're speaking to yourself.

_____
_____
_____
_____
_____
_____

FAITH CLINIC-VOLUME VI-GRIEF CLINIC EDITION

6. **What one declaration from above do you most need to repeat daily this week?** Write it big and bold across this page.

Closing Note

This chapter is not about fireworks faith. It's about the slow, steady, stubborn act of showing up. Feelings will return, but faith is what you build in silence. Numbness is not failure — it is evidence that you're still alive, still breathing, still holding on.

"Even when your faith feels numb and your hallelujah is hollow, God still hears the silent ache of your soul."

-DR. PATRICIA S. TANNER

Chapter 8

Guilt, Regrets & The "What-If's"

SYMPTOM

🩺 EMOTIONAL LOOPS OF GUILT & SELF-BLAME

Your mind replays the past like a broken record—fixating on what you could have done, said, or changed. You're stuck in a mental cycle of regret, questioning decisions and rehearsing moments you can't undo. Grief latches onto guilt, dragging your heart into shame and torment.

Grief doesn't just bring sadness — it drags guilt into the room like an uninvited guest that won't stop talking. For many, it's not just the loss itself that hurts, it's the echo of *what could have been*. You replay the last conversation you had with your loved one, or worse, the one you never got to have. The "what ifs" keep you up at night. *What if I had answered. that call? What if I had visited more? What if I had told them I loved them one more time? What if I had done something differently — would they still be here?*

These thoughts become a mental prison. Instead of memories bringing comfort, they can morph into accusations: *You failed them. You weren t enough. You didn t do enough.* And while grief alone is heavy, guilt straps cinderblocks to your soul.

What makes this symptom so tormenting is how it weaponizes love. You feel guilty because you cared. You feel regret because you wanted more time. You punish yourself because, deep down, you believe your love should have been enough to stop death itself. But let's be clear: you're human, not God. You couldn't't control sickness, accidents, or time. Yet guilt whispers that somehow you should have been able to.

The danger of carrying guilt in grief is that it keeps you stuck in a loop of *rewinding* instead of living. Instead of moving forward in healing, you rehearse regrets like they're your personal playlist of shame. And every track ends the same way — with condemnation.

This is the symptom: grief complicated by guilt. You can't change the past, but the past keeps changing you — unless you learn to release it.

 GRIEF CLINIC TOOLKIT

Tool To Reverse Guilt: Romans 8:1

The enemy loves to twist grief into guilt. He takes what was meant to be love and remembrance, and he distorts it into shame and condemnation. But here's the truth: *Therefore, there is now no condemnation for those who are in Christ Jesus"* (**Romans 8:1, NIV**).

That verse isn't just about salvation — it's about living free from the weight of self-punishment. When you belong to Christ, you don't get to carry both the cross and your own personal execution chair. Jesus already carried the guilt. He already bore the regret. He already took the condemnation. Yet grief tricks us into thinking, *Sure, Jesus forgives sin — but He probably won't forgive me for not being enough when it mattered most.*

That's a lie.

Your salvation wasn't earned by being "enough," and neither is your healing in grief. The truth is, none of us will ever do this life perfectly. You weren't meant to. Death is always going to feel unfinished, because human love is infinite in desire and finite in time. There will always be one more word you wish you could have said, one more hug you wish you could have given, one more day you wish you had. That doesn't mean you failed — it means you're human.

The tool for your toolkit is simple but revolutionary: grief will try to trap you in condemnation, but the cross has already released you from it. Regret will whisper that your mistakes define the legacy of your loved one, but God's mercy says otherwise. Their life was not summed up by your final words. Their death was not determined by your actions.

What you need to know is this: God doesn't hold you on trial for the "what ifs." He holds you in mercy for the "what is." And the "what is" is this — He is present, He is healer, and He is the one who writes the last chapter, not you.

FAITH PRESCRIPTION

Take these verses as your prescription — not a spiritual band-aid, but a healing truth to digest daily:

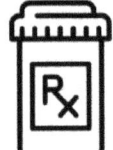

☐ *Therefore, there is now no condemnation for those who are in Christ Jesus."* — **Romans 8:1 (NIV)**

☐ *Cast all your anxiety on him because he cares for you."* — **1 Peter 5:7 (NIV)**

☐ *As far as the east is from the west, so far has he removed our transgressions from us."* — **Psalm 103:12 (NIV)**

These verses are not "nice quotes" — they are medicine for your tormented soul. Read them, write them, repeat them, until the lie of condemnation gets drowned out by the truth of God's mercy.

🔹 SPIRITUAL VITAMIN

Vitamin RG for Release Guilt: *Mercy is greater than memory.*

Take it daily. Every time guilt replays a memory with a false verdict, you remind yourself: God's mercy is bigger. His cross already covered not only your sin, but your shortcomings, your silence, your missed moments, your "what ifs."

Just like your body can't survive without vitamins, your soul can't survive grief without mercy; take mercy as a vitamin. Keep swallowing the truth that you are not condemned.

🔹 HOLY SPIRIT CONSULT

Think of the Holy Spirit as your grief counselor who knows the end of the story. He's the one who whispers comfort when guilt shouts condemnation. In **John 14:26**, Jesus calls Him "the Helper" — and part of His job is to remind you of truth when your emotions start lying.

Here's how the consult sounds: *Child, you loved them. Even in your imperfection, you loved them. I was there in the words you never got to say. I was present at the moments you missed. I am the God of mercy, and I hold both you and your loved one in My eternal hands. Stop carrying what I already covered.*

When guilt rises, invite the Spirit to speak louder than your memory. Ask Him to reinterpret your regrets through the lens of grace. He will.

🙏 Guided Prayer + Declarations

"Father, I admit I am carrying guilt I was never meant to carry. I've replayed moments, conversations, and choices, and I feel trapped in the "what ifs." Forgive me for believing the lie that I should have been enough to change what only You control.

Lord, I release my regrets into Your mercy. Cover the unfinished parts of my grief with Your grace. Silence the enemy's accusations and replace them with Your peace. Thank You for reminding me that there is no condemnation in You. Help me walk in freedom, even as I heal in grief. Amen."

Faith Declarations:

1. I declare that guilt does not define me — God's mercy does.

2. I declare that I am free from condemnation in Christ.

3. I declare that my regrets are not stronger than God's redemption.

4. I declare that the "what ifs" will not torment me; I release them into God's hands.

5. I declare that grief will not hold me hostage to self-punishment.

6. I declare that God's mercy rewrites every memory with grace.

7. I declare that I am forgiven, free, and fully loved by God.

8. I declare that my loved one's story is not diminished by my imperfection.

9. I declare that I will live without torment because Jesus already bore my condemnation.

10. I declare that healing is mine, and mercy is my daily portion.

📝 Journal + Reflection Page

✏️ Use this page to process what guilt has tried to steal from you.

1. **Write down one "what if" that keeps haunting you.**

   _____
   _____
   _____
   _____
   _____
   _____
   _____
   _____
   _____
   _____
   _____

2. **Now, write a truth from scripture (Romans 8:1, Psalm 103:12) to cancel that lie.**

   _____
   _____
   _____
   _____

3. Think of one memory with your loved one that brings joy instead of guilt. Write it in detail and thank God for it.

4. Write a letter to yourself as if Jesus were speaking. What would He say about your guilt?

5. **List one small step you can take this week to release regret into God's hands (prayer, burning a note of guilt, speaking a declaration daily).**

▶ Closing Note

Grief will always whisper "what if," but God's mercy will always shout "enough." Your love was real. Your presence mattered. And your healing is possible when you stop carrying guilt that Christ already carried to the cross.

"Regret is a robber that tries to steal what's left after loss. But grace is a restorer— reminding you that even in your worst 'what-if,' God still sees your heart."

-Dr. PATRICIA S. TANNER

FAITH CLINIC-VOLUME VI-GRIEF CLINIC EDITION

Chapter 9

Healing Doesn't Mean Forgetting

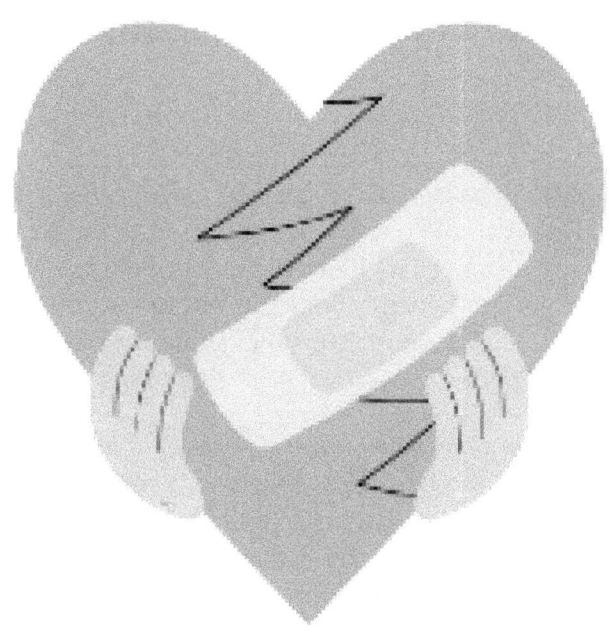

DR. PATRICIA S. TANNER

SYMPTOM

⚕ PHYSICAL DUISRUPTION OF ROUTINE & VITAL RYTHMS

Grief doesn't just ache in the heart—it rattles the body. You may lose your appetite or binge to fill a void. Sleep becomes irregular—either elusive or excessive. Energy levels swing from numb fatigue to restlessness, making even basic routines feel like mountain climbing.

The Fear Of Moving Forward — Why Joy Can Feel Like Betrayal

One of the strangest symptoms of grief is the guilt you feel when joy tries to sneak back into your life. You catch yourself laughing at a movie, enjoying dinner with friends, or feeling a spark of excitement about the future — and then shame sucker-punches you. *How dare you be happy? Don t you care? Aren t you forgetting them?*

This is the hidden fear of moving forward: that healing equals betrayal. It feels like if you let the tears slow down, if you start living again, you're leaving your loved one behind. So, you keep yourself in an emotional holding cell, afraid that joy means disloyalty. The unspoken belief is: *If I keep hurting, it proves how much I loved them. If I smile, maybe it proves I didn t.*

But that s a lie grief tells.

The truth is that grief and joy are not enemies. You can carry both — pain and laughter, sadness and hope — in the same heart. Healing doesn't dishonor their memory; it honors it. Staying frozen in sorrow doesn't prove your love, it only proves your captivity. Love was never meant to be chained to misery. If you've ever felt guilty for feeling good, you're not crazy — you're grieving. But you don't have to live stuck in that symptom.

🧰 GRIEF CLINIC TOOLKIT 🧰

Tool To Move Forward: Isaiah 43:19

Love doesn't die just because the body does. Grief proves that. Your tears are proof of love's endurance, and your memories are proof that death cannot erase what God wrote in your soul. But here's where we often stumble: we confuse memory with identity. We think if we stop carrying grief like a weight, we stop carrying them at all.

But your loved one's story doesn't need you trapped to validate it. You are not the sum of their absence. You are still *you* — the one God made in His image, the one He still has plans for, the one who is allowed to laugh, breathe, and live. Healing doesn't mean you cut ties with their memory; it means you stop confusing grief with loyalty.

Think about Jesus. When He visited Mary and Martha after Lazarus' death, He wept (**John 11:35**). He entered their grief — but then He also raised Lazarus. That moment showed us something profound: love is not just about mourning the grave; it's about bringing life even after loss.

Healing gives you permission to carry memory differently. Instead of wearing grief like shackles, you wear it like a necklace — something that's with you, but not something that chains you. You can remember without reliving trauma. You can honor without being held hostage. Love beyond the grave is not about forgetting them; it's about remembering them with hope instead of only hurt.

When Jesus rose from the dead, He didn't come back polished and flawless. He came back with scars. In **John 20:27**, He invited Thomas to touch His wounds — evidence that resurrection doesn't erase pain, it transforms it.

This is the tool for your toolkit: your healing will still carry marks. You may always have moments where the loss aches, where a song triggers tears, where a memory cracks open your chest. That doesn't mean you're not healed. That means you're human.

Jesus showed us that wholeness and wounds can live in the same body. Resurrection doesn't erase the past; it redefines it. Your scars aren't proof of failure — they're proof of survival. And in the Kingdom, scars become testimonies.

So don't expect healing to erase everything. Expect it to *redeem* everything. You will carry both grief and growth, both memory and movement. That's not betrayal — that's resurrection life.

FAITH PRESCRIPTION

Take this as your prescription:

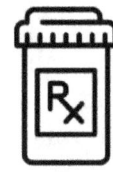

☐ *There is a time to weep and a time to laugh, a time to mourn and a time to dance."* — **Ecclesiastes 3:4 (NIV)**

☐ *The Lord is close to the brokenhearted and saves those who are crushed in spirit."* — **Psalm 34:18 (NIV)**

> *See, I am doing a new thing! Now it springs up; do you not perceive it?"* — **Isaiah 43:19 (NIV)**

God never asked you to forget. He asked you to heal. Healing doesn't erase memory; it reshapes it. Every smile you allow yourself to feel isn't betrayal — it's testimony that grief is real, but so is life after grief.

💊 SPIRITUAL VITAMIN

Vitamin H for Healing: *Joy is not betrayal — it's proof of survival.*

Take this daily. Every time you feel guilty for laughing, remind yourself: your loved one's life is honored not by your torment, but by your ability to live on with gratitude.

🕊 HOLY SPIRIT CONSULT

The Holy Spirit doesn't shame you for smiling. He whispers reassurance: *Your healing doesn't erase them. It honors them. Your laughter doesn't abandon their memory. It testifies of My comfort. I was with them in their last breath, and I am with you in every new one. Healing doesn't mean forgetting — it means you're finally free to carry them without breaking under the weight."*

The Spirit isn't asking you to let go of love — He's asking you to let go of the chains of guilt around it.

🙏 Guided Prayer + Declarations

"Father, I confess I've been afraid that moving forward means leaving my loved one behind. I've carried guilt for laughing, for smiling, for enjoying life again.

Lord, remind me that healing doesn't erase love — it deepens it. Help me carry memories without shame, and scars without despair. Thank You for showing me through Jesus' scars that resurrection doesn't mean forgetting, it means transforming. I chose today to honor their life by living mine. In Jesus' name, Amen."

Faith Declarations:

1. I declare that healing honors memory, not erases it.
2. I declare that joy is not betrayal, but survival.
3. I declare that my scars are proof of resurrection, not failure.
4. I declare that I can carry memory without losing identity.
5. I declare that love goes beyond the grave.
6. I declare that I will not confuse grief with loyalty.
7. I declare that Jesus' resurrection proves wounds and healing can coexist.
8. I declare that my loved one's life is honored in my healing, not my torment.
9. I declare that I am free to move forward without shame.
10. I declare that healing is holy, and joy is a gift from God.

 Journal + Reflection Page

Take a few minutes with these prompts:

FAITH CLINIC-VOLUME VI-GRIEF CLINIC EDITION

1. **Write down one moment of guilt you've felt for experiencing joy since your loss.** Now reframe it — how could that joy actually honor their memory?

   _____
   _____
   _____
   _____
   _____
   _____
   _____
   _____

2. **Reflect on Jesus 'scars. How do your own emotional "scars" prove both pain and survival?** Write one way your scars can testify of hope.

   _____
   _____
   _____
   _____
   _____
   _____
   _____
   _____

3. List three ways you can carry your loved one's memory in life-giving ways (ex: traditions, stories, acts of service, photos, art).

_____
_____
_____
_____
_____
_____
_____
_____

4. Write a prayer to your future self, reminding you that healing is not betrayal.

_____
_____
_____
_____
_____
_____
_____
_____

5. Describe what "living forward" could look like for you without shame.

FAITH CLINIC-VOLUME VI-GRIEF CLINIC EDITION

Closing Note

Healing doesn't ask you to forget. It asks you to *remember differently.* You can carry memory without carrying condemnation. You can move forward without leaving love behind. And when joy comes again, don't see it as betrayal — see it as resurrection.

DR. PATRICIA S. TANNER

"Grief changes form, but never erases love. Healing is the grace to remember without unraveling."

-DR. PATRICIA S. TANNER

FAITH CLINIC-VOLUME VI-GRIEF CLINIC EDITION

Chapter 10

Still Breathing, Still Called

DR. PATRICIA S. TANNER

📋 SYMPTOM

🩺 NUMBNESS THAT MASKS PURPOSE

In the haze of grief, the ability to dream again feels suffocated. You're alive but not living—breathing but barely believing. The call of God feels distant beneath the weight of sorrow, and you may question whether your purpose still matters in a world without them.

One of the heaviest weights in grief is what people rarely talk about: survivors' guilt. You wake up every morning with the reminder that you are still breathing while the one you love is not. And that reality doesn't just ache — it accuses.

Thoughts creep in: *Why them and not me? Why am I here, and they're gone?*

That guilt can freeze you in place. It can make you feel like life is unfair in ways you don't know how to explain. On some days, it feels wrong to enjoy what they can't. On other days, you might even feel resentful of your own breath. You wonder if being alive is a gift or a burden.

But here's the truth — survivor's guilt is not a sentence from God. It's the side effect of a broken world colliding with love. Your breath is not an accident. If you're here, it's because God still has a plan that requires your presence. The very fact that you're still alive means Heaven still trusts you with a mission.

So, while survivor's guilt feels like a chain, God sees your breath as evidence of assignment. You are not here by mistake. You are still breathing because you are still called.

 GRIEF CLINIC TOOLKIT

Tool To Answer The Call: Jeremiah 29:11

Grief has a way of convincing you that your story ended with theirs. That because their chapter closed, yours has no plot left to unfold. But the Word of God insists otherwise.

Jeremiah 29:11 (NIV) says, *"For I know the plans I have for you… plans to prosper you and not to harm you, plans to give you hope and a future."* Notice that this was written to people in exile, people who felt abandoned and broken, much like you might now. God didn't wait for them to be comfortable to speak hope. He declared purpose *in the middle of their pain.*

Your grief does not disqualify you from God's plan. In fact, your pain often becomes the soil for your calling. Think about Moses: a murderer turned deliverer. Think about Joseph: betrayed, imprisoned, but still elevated for God's glory. Think about Jesus: despised, rejected, crucified — and yet His suffering became the greatest redemption story.

If God used pain as the birthplace of their assignments, why wouldn't He do the same with you? Your purpose didn't die when your loved one did. If anything, your pain sharpened it.

Grief gives you two choices: you can let it silence you, or you can let it speak. Legacy living means choosing the second option. It means turning the ache into an anthem. It means telling the story of how love shaped you, how loss broke you, and how God is still putting you back together.

Legacy doesn't mean you set up a statue or build a shrine. It means you live in a way that reflects what they meant to you. It's in the kindness you show because they taught you compassion. It's in the risks you take because they believed in your courage. It's in the way you speak their name not just with sorrow, but with gratitude.

Think of **Hebrews 12:1 (NIV)**: *"Therefore, since we are surrounded by such a great cloud of witnesses... let us run with perseverance the race marked out for us."* That cloud of witnesses is cheering you on. Your loved one's memory is not a weight keeping you down — it's a wind pushing you forward.

Legacy living says: *I refuse to let their life end in silence. I will carry what they taught me into what God is still writing through me.*

FAITH PRESCRIPTION

Here's the hard truth: closure is a myth. You won't wake up one day and find grief neatly wrapped with a bow, pain erased, and all questions answered. That's not how love works, and that's not how loss heals.

But calling? That's real. And it's waiting for you.

📖 *"The gifts and the calling of God are irrevocable."* — **Romans 11:29 (NIV)**

📖 *"For we are God's handiwork, created in Christ Jesus to do good works, which God prepared in advance for us to do."* — **Ephesians 2:10 (NIV)**

FAITH CLINIC-VOLUME VI-GRIEF CLINIC EDITION

"You did not choose me, but I chose you and appointed you so that you might go and bear fruit — fruit that will last." — **John 15:16 (NIV)**

Stop exhausting yourself looking for closure. Instead, embrace your calling. Closure won't heal you — but calling will give your pain a place to land.

🔖 SPIRITUAL VITAMIN

Vitamin S for Survivors: *Breath means assignment. If I'm alive, God's not done.*

Take this daily. Every inhale is proof you still have purpose.

🕊 HOLY SPIRIT CONSULT

The Holy Spirit whispers: *"I did not make a mistake keeping you here. Your life is not random. Your breath is not wasted. I will turn your mourning into mission, your pain into purpose, your grief into grace for others. Don't waste your life waiting for closure. Step into calling. Because you are still breathing, you are still chosen."*

🙏 Guided Prayer + Declarations

"Father, thank You that my breath is proof I still matter to You. I confess I've wrestled with survivor's guilt, wondering why I'm here and they're not. But today, I choose to believe that my life is intentional, not accidental.

Give me courage to embrace the calling You've placed on me, even in the middle of grief. Help me live as a legacy, not just a mourner. I don't need closure — I need courage to step into purpose. Thank You that my pain is not wasted. In Jesus' name, Amen."

Faith Declarations

1. I declare that my breath is proof of my assignment.

2. I declare that God's plan for me is alive, even in grief.

3. I declare that my loved one's memory fuels my mission.

4. I declare that I will not chase closure — I will embrace calling.

5. I declare that legacy is how I honor, not how I stay chained.

6. I declare that survivor's guilt is replaced with survivor's purpose.

7. I declare that every scar can tell a story of God's grace.

8. I declare that my life still carries fruit God ordained.

9. I declare that grief will not paralyze me — it will propel me.

10. I declare that I am still breathing because I am still called.

📝 Journal + Reflection Page

✒ *Reflect on these prompts:*

1. **When have you felt the sting of survivor's guilt?** Write down what made you feel guilty for still being here.

_____
_____
_____
_____

FAITH CLINIC-VOLUME VI-GRIEF CLINIC EDITION

2. How could that guilt shift into gratitude — gratitude that you still have breath and purpose?

3. Write one way you can live out a legacy that honors your loved one's life.

4. **What part of God's calling have you put on pause because of grief?** How can you restart today?

_____
_____
_____
_____
_____
_____
_____

5. **Finish this sentence:** *Because I'm still breathing, I will…*

_____
_____
_____
_____
_____
_____
_____

Closing Note

Closure is overrated. Calling is eternal. Your loved one's life mattered, but so does yours. You're still here because God's still writing. Stop apologizing for your breath — and start living it.

FAITH CLINIC-VOLUME VI-GRIEF CLINIC EDITION

Epilogue

I'm Not Ok, But I'm Still Here

~ *Grief Clinic Discharge Plan* ~

Let's be honest. If you've made it this far in this book, you know that grief is not neat, polished, or easy to package into "five stages." It's messy. It's unpredictable. It's ugly crying in the middle of grocery store aisles because you saw something that reminded you of them. It's laughing at a memory one minute and collapsing into tears the next. It's being okay enough to go to work on Tuesday but broken enough that you can't get out of bed on Wednesday.

So, let's start here: you don't have to be okay right now.

That may sound strange at the end of a book about healing, but it's the truest place to begin. Healing doesn't mean pretending you're fine when you're not. Healing doesn't mean you've arrived at some magical finish line where pain no longer exists. Healing simply means you're still here. Still breathing. Still standing — even if it's shaky. Still walking — even if it's slow. Still living — even if it doesn't always feel like life.

And that in itself is a miracle.

Owning Your Reality:
Not Healed Overnight, Not Hopeless Either

One of the cruelest lies grief tells you is that because you're not "better" by now, you never will be. People might even add to the pressure with their well-meaning but hurtful words: *"It's time to move on."* Or *"Haven't you healed yet?"* But you don't move on from love. You don't just close the book on someone who shaped your life.

The truth is: you're not healed overnight, but you're not hopeless either. Healing takes time — and sometimes, a lifetime.

Think about the disciples after Jesus died. They hid in fear, locked in an upper room, overwhelmed by grief. They didn't heal instantly. They didn't suddenly understand what God was doing. They wrestled. They doubted. They even gave up for a time. But God didn't abandon them in that locked room. He met them there. He showed up in their fear, their confusion, their sorrow.

And He'll do the same for you.

Owning your reality means admitting: *"I'm not okay today."* And guess what? That doesn't make you faithless — it makes you honest. Faith doesn't deny pain; it holds onto God in the middle of it. You're allowed to cry, to question, to fall apart, and still believe that God is holding you together.

The Long Walk:
Healing Is A Lifelong Process, Not A Deadline

Grief isn't something you get over. It's something you learn to carry. Some days it feels lighter, some days it feels like a mountain on your chest. But healing is not a race to the finish line. It's a long walk — one step at a time.

Abraham waited decades for God's promises. Joseph endured years of betrayal and prison before he saw redemption. The Israelites wandered forty years before entering the promised land. God's timing rarely fits human schedules. Healing, too, is not rushed.

And that's good news. Why? Because it means there's no deadline for your progress. You don't have to "get over it" in six months, one year, or even ten. You don't have to measure your worth by how fast you smile again. Healing is not about speed — it's about direction. Are you moving, even slowly, toward hope? Then you are healing.

Even Jesus showed us that wounds don't just vanish. After His resurrection, He still had scars. Scars don't mean failure. Scars mean survival. Scars mean you've walked through the fire and lived to tell the story.

Give yourself permission to walk slowly. Healing isn't about how quickly you get there; it's about learning how to keep walking with God as your companion.

Faith Anchors: God's Grace In Every Stage Of Grief

When the storm of grief rages, you need an anchor. Something that holds you in place when the waves try to pull you under. That anchor is not denial. That anchor is not pretending you're fine. That anchor is God's grace.

Paul said in **2 Corinthians 12:9**, *"My grace is sufficient for you, for my power is made perfect in weakness."* Notice what God didn't say. He didn't say, "My grace will remove all your pain." He didn't say, "My grace will erase your grief." He said, *"My grace is sufficient."* That means His grace is enough to carry you through every stage — even the messy ones.

Grace meets you when you're angry at God and don't want to pray. Grace meets you when you're too numb to worship. Grace meets you when you can't stop crying. Grace meets you in silence. Grace meets you in chaos.

And grace whispers: *"You don't have to have it all together. I've got you."*

Every stage of grief — denial, anger, bargaining, depression, acceptance — is a place where grace shows up. And grace doesn't just sit with you; grace strengthens you to keep moving. Grace says, *"Even here, you are not alone."*

Final Call: Hope Is Not Denial — It's Survival

Hope gets a bad reputation in grief. People think hope means pretending everything's fine, slapping on a fake smile, or refusing to acknowledge pain. That's not hope — that's denial.

Real hope looks like this: you admit your heart is broken, and you still believe God can heal it. You confess you don't have all the answers, and you still trust the One who does. You say, *"I'm not okay, but I'm still here."* That's not weakness. That's faith.

Hope is what keeps you breathing when depression whispers that life isn't worth it. Hope is what keeps you alive when anxiety screams that tomorrow will be worse than today. Hope is what reminds you that pain is real, but so is purpose.

If you're reading this and suicide has crossed your mind, I need you to hear this clearly: **don't quit now**. Don't believe the lie that the world would be better without you. Don't let grief convince you your life is over. If you're still breathing, God still has a calling for you.

Psalm 118:17 says, *"I will not die but live, and will proclaim what the Lord has done."* That verse is not just ink on a page — it's your declaration. You are alive for a reason. You are here for a purpose. And hope is not naïve — hope is your lifeline.

Bringing It All Together

Every chapter in this book has walked you through the symptoms of grief, the tools from the scripture, and the prescriptions of faith. From the shock of loss to the torment of guilt, to the fear of forgetting, to the survivor's reality — every page has carried one truth: ***you are not abandoned in your grief.***

God is not afraid of your questions. He is not distant from your pain. He is close to the brokenhearted (**Psalm 34:18**). He bottles your tears (**Psalm 56:8**). He promises that joy will come in the morning (**Psalm 30:5**), even if the night feels endless.

You are not okay right now. That's fine. You are not hopeless either. That's a miracle.

Healing won't erase your scars, but it will remind you that scars are signs of survival. Healing won't silence your grief, but it will give you grace to live alongside it. Healing won't bring them back, but it will bring you forward.

A Final Word For You

You are not reading this by accident. If you've wrestled with suicidal thoughts, if you've battled depression so heavy you can't see tomorrow, if grief has made you believe that life is not worth living — hear me: *you are still here*. And that matters. You are still here because heaven still has a role for you. You are still here because love isn't finished with your story. You are still here because God is not done.

This book isn't your finish line. It's your checkpoint. A reminder that grief didn't erase your worth, your calling, or your hope. Healing may take a lifetime, but you've already proven something grief couldn't steal: your survival.

So don't quit. Don't give in to the lie that says, "This is it." No — this is *not* it. This is not the end. This is the valley before the mountain. This is the scar before the testimony. This is the crack in the shell before the light gets through.

You don't have to be okay. You just have to keep being here. And that's enough.

If you've ever felt like ending your life, I want you to pause and hear me: ***you are worth staying.*** The world is not better without you. The Kingdom of God is not complete without your voice. Your story is not over, even if this chapter feels unbearable. God still calls you by name. God still has plans for your life. God still writes new pages for your story.

And if all you can say today is, *"I'm not okay, but I'm still here,"* that's enough. Heaven cheers at that kind of faith. That's survival. That's strength. That's the seed of hope.

So, breathe. Take one step. Cry if you need to. Rest if you must. But don't quit. Your scars will tell a story of survival. Your pain will birth a testimony of purpose. And your life — yes, ***your*** life — will still give glory to God.

Because you're still breathing. And you're still called.

Faith Prescription: Hope Is Oxygen, Not Denial

- **Step 1: Own the truth.** Stop pretending you're okay. Confession breaks shame's hold. Say it out loud: "I'm not okay, but I'm not quitting."

- **Step 2: Anchor in grace.** Write **Hebrews 13:5** on your mirror: *"Never will I leave you; never will I forsake you."* Every morning, remind yourself that grief shifts, but God doesn't.

- **Step 3: Trade deadlines for daily bread.** Healing doesn't come by circling a date on the calendar. It comes by choosing God's presence one day, one breath, one tear at a time.

- **Step 4: Practice survival hope.** Hope doesn't deny pain; it dares to live *through* pain. Whisper it daily: *"Hope is not denial — it's survival."*

💊 SPIRITUAL VITAMIN: "Still Standing Supplement"

Take this spiritual supplement daily:

- **Vitamin Verse — Lamentations 3:22–23**

  "Because of the Lord's great love we are not consumed, for his compassions never fail. They are new every morning; great is your faithfulness."

- **Dosage:** Every morning, before scrolling social media or drowning in your thoughts, repeat this: *"I am not consumed. His mercies meet me fresh today."*

- **Side Effects:** You may experience unexpected moments of peace, strength in weakness, and the ability to breathe even in the heaviness.

🕊️ HOLY SPIRIT CONSULT
When You Can't Fix It, Let Him Hold It

In medicine, consultations happen when the doctor brings in a specialist. In your grief, the Holy Spirit is your divine specialist. **Romans 8:26** reminds us that when we don't even know what to pray, the Spirit intercedes with groans too deep for words.

That means your sighs, your silence, your "God, I can't" are enough. The Spirit translates them into a heavenly language that moves the heart of the Father. Stop disqualifying your weak prayers. The Holy Spirit is filling in the blanks.

🙏 Guided Prayer + Declarations

Prayer:
"Father, I admit I am not okay. My heart is heavy, my faith feels fragile, but I refuse to quit. Thank You for holding me together when I am unraveling. Thank You for giving me breath when I don't want to breathe. Anchor me in Your grace when waves of grief rise.

Help me to believe that surviving today is enough. Jesus, walk with me in this valley, and let Your scars remind me that resurrection is still possible for me too. Amen."

Declarations (Say these out loud daily):

- I am not hopeless, even when I feel broken.

- Healing is not a deadline — it's a journey, and I'm still walking.

- My survival is proof that God isn't done with me.

- Hope is not denial — it's my oxygen.

- I'm not okay, but I'm still here. And that's enough.

📓 Journal + Reflection Page

1. **What lies has grief whispered to me about being "done?"**

_____
_____
_____
_____

2. What Scriptures or truths can I anchor myself to when I feel like quitting?

3. How has God shown me that my survival still matters?

FAITH CLINIC-VOLUME VI-GRIEF CLINIC EDITION

_____
_____

4. Write down one reason you're still here today — no matter how small.

_____
_____
_____
_____
_____
_____

5. What would it look like to honor my grief while still choosing to live?

_____
_____
_____
_____
_____
_____
_____
_____
_____
_____

DR. PATRICIA S. TANNER

✦ FINAL CALL TO READER

Don't chase closure — chase calling. Don't wait for perfect healing before you live. The fact that you're still breathing means heaven still has use for you. You don't have to be okay. You just have to keep being here. And that is more than enough.

Faith Clinic Discharge Plan

(Your Aftercare for the Grieving Soul)

Patient Name: _____

Date of Release: _____

Attending Physician: Dr. Jesus Christ, The Great Physician

Treatment Summary: You entered the Faith Clinic weighed down with grief, depression, anxiety, regret, and hopelessness. Through God's Word, prayer, and His Spirit, you've received prescriptions of hope, spiritual vitamins of truth, and the reassurance that healing is possible. You are not fully discharged from pain — but you are equipped to survive, breathe, and rebuild.

Aftercare Instructions

1. Daily Check-Ins with God (Prayer + Word)

- Begin your morning with one scripture (start with **Psalm 34:18, Lamentations 3:22–23, or John 11:25**).

- Whisper at least one honest sentence to God daily. Even if it's just: *"God, I need You today."*

- Don't aim for perfection; aim for presence.

2. Medication: The Word of God

Take these daily doses:

- **Morning: Psalm 23** — to remind yourself you're not walking alone.

- **Afternoon: Romans 8:1** — no condemnation in Christ.

- **Night: Revelation 21:4** — one day, no more tears or death.

3. Activity Restrictions

- Avoid isolation completely. It's okay to rest, but don't starve your soul of connection.

- Limit doom-scrolling social media if it fuels guilt, comparison, or hopelessness.

- Do not engage in self-harming behaviors. Replace the urge with journaling, calling someone safe, or praying raw prayers.

4. Follow-Up Appointments

- **Weekly Check-In:** With a trusted friend, mentor, or grief support group.

- **Monthly Review:** Journal your progress: *"Where was I last month compared to today?"*

- **Emergency Appointment:** Call on God immediately when suicidal thoughts or overwhelming darkness creep in. He is on-call 24/7.

5. *Warning Signs — When to Seek Immediate Help*

If you experience:

- Persistent suicidal thoughts.
- Complete withdrawal from loved ones.
- Inability to eat, sleep, or care for yourself.
- Thoughts of harming yourself or others.

📞 **Call 988 (Suicide & Crisis Lifeline)** in the U.S. For readers outside the U.S., look up your local crisis hotline now and write it here: _____.

You don't have to fight alone. Emergency help is not a lack of faith — it's a lifeline God can use.

Spiritual Prescriptions For Survival

- **Faith Prescription:** Stop chasing closure, start embracing calling.
- **Spiritual Vitamin:** *"Because of the Lord's great love we are not consumed..."* (**Lamentations 3:22–23**).
- **Holy Spirit Consult:** Let Him intercede when you have no words
- **Guided Prayer:** *"Lord, I'm not okay, but I'm still here. Keep me breathing, keep me believing."*

Lifestyle Recommendations

- **Move your body.** A 10-minute walk counts.

- **Rest when you need to.** Elijah was given sleep and food before instructions.

- **Talk to others.** Community is a treatment, not an option.

- **Honor your loved one.** Write letters, create memory rituals, or serve in their honor.

Discharge Affirmations

Repeat daily:

- I am not alone in this grief.
- I can feel broken and still be loved.
- My pain does not cancel my purpose.
- Healing is not forgetting; it's learning to live again.
- I am still here, which means God is not finished with me.

Next Steps

- ☑ Journal your progress.
- ☑ Stay connected to your support system.
- ☑ Read scripture as medicine, not homework.
- ☑ Keep showing up — one day, one breath at a time.

For ongoing support, I would love to meet you in my coaching program-Just Grieve. It is a week program where I walk you through the 30 days of grieving and provide an outlet for you to put the message of this grief clinic in action.

You can gain support from others who are grieving, yet learning how to cope with their loss in a positive and loving environment. I would love to meet you and share in your story of hope and survival. To learn more about this program, visit my ministry website: **https://www.7sevenworld.com/challenges**.

Final Call

This discharge does not mean you're "fixed." It means you're equipped. You are not released into emptiness — you are released into *purpose, grace, and ongoing healing.*

📌 *Remember*: *Healing is not denial. It's survival. And survival is proof of God's mercy at work in your story.*

"Survival in the shadow of sorrow is still survival. You don't have to be okay to be present, you just have to breathe and believe healing will meet you where you are."

-DR. PATRICIA S. TANNER

ABOUT THE AUTHOR

Dr. Patricia Tanner was born and raised in Sanford FL. She comes from a family of three siblings. Patricia Tanner is the founder of Multhai International Realty, Multhai Asset Management Services, and Multhai Investment Group which is located in Sanford, Florida. She is a graduate of the University of Central Florida, where she received a Bachelor of Science in Business Administration and a minor in Human Resources Management.

Dr. Tanner began her career shortly thereafter as a Regional Property Manager in the apartment community. Throughout her career in property management, she has built interpersonal relationships with corporate clients. She has a successful track record of increasing company revenues over $5 million annually, through hard work, commitment, creativeness, and strategic planning.

Her experience and leadership role eventually led her to achieve a Florida Real Estate Broker license. She spent fifteen years in the Real Estate field while completing a Master of Arts in Human Resources Management from Webster University, and a Master of Public Administration from Troy University. It was in this capacity that she decided to open her own brokerage company, Multhai International Realty.

In addition, Dr. Tanner finds time in her busy schedule to participate in her own Non-For-Profit Organization, Stones 2 Homes. She remains President of her organization in which she helps people build, keep, or purchase homes in affordable communities. She is the founder of PNT Property Partners in which she buys vacant land, develops it, and constructs brand new construction homes in Sanford Florida. Her overall goal is to educate and provide resources to help people overcome financial hardships and credit disadvantage to live the American Dream through homeownership in spite of economic hardship. Through her visions she will continue to grow as an entrepreneur and is willing to share her knowledge, experience, and expertise with anyone who is willing to learn.

MORE BOOKS BY THE AUTHOR

Welcome to the Faith Clinic—where your soul doesn't need to be perfect to be healed.

You've smiled through burnout. Quoted scripture while quietly unraveling. Prayed, fasted, and still felt like your faith flatlined. If that's you, Faith Clinic: Volume I is your spiritual prescription.

Dr. Patricia S. Tanner—known as The Faith Doctor—invites you into a raw, grace-filled recovery journey for the soul. With 7 powerful doses of faith-infused wisdom, this book delivers healing where performance failed and offers truth where church hurt left a scar. Designed especially for spiritually exhausted youth and young adults, each "dose" reads like an IV drip of hope for believers secretly running on empty.

You don't need to be okay to show up. You just need to be willing. The clinic is open.

NOW AVAILABLE:
www.amazon.com

DR. PATRICIA S. TANNER

Healing was just the beginning. Now it's time to grow.

If Faith Clinic Volume I met you in crisis, Volume II meets you in recovery. Because faith isn't a one-time fix—it's a lifestyle that needs maintenance, accountability, and consistency. Welcome to your follow-up care plan.

In Faith Clinic: Volume II, Dr. Patricia S. Tanner—aka The Faith Doctor—guides you through the next level of your spiritual healing journey. From navigating church trauma and burnout to facing silence from God and rediscovering purpose, this book goes deeper than devotionals. It's not about hype—it's about habits that sustain real, lasting transformation.

With raw wisdom, relatable stories, and no-shame truths, each chapter is a spiritual check-in for believers who want to thrive—not just survive. Whether you're wrestling with doubt, craving stability, or simply ready to grow up in God, this clinic is for you.

You've detoxed. Now it's time to build. Let's get you discharge-ready.

NOW AVAILABLE:
www.amazon.com

FAITH CLINIC-VOLUME VI-GRIEF CLINIC EDITION

Welcome to the Faith Clinic: Anxiety Edition — where God doesn't coddle your coping mechanisms but confronts them with surgical precision.

This book is for the ones who love Jesus but still can't sleep. For the worship leaders crying in church bathrooms. For the believers who pray in spirals, fight shame on Sundays, and secretly think, "Maybe I'm the only one who can't seem to breathe through this." You're not crazy. You're just in a fight — and this book is your spiritual triage.

Inside you'll find:
- ☑ Panic attacks in pews and the prayers that still work.
- ☑ Scriptures that talk you off the ledge.
- ☑ What to do when you feel numb and God feels quiet.
- ☑ How to walk out of shame loops, judgment spirals, and performance religion.

This isn't just encouragement. It's equipment.
Because healing isn't a moment — it's a walk.

NOW AVAILABLE:
www.amazon.com

DR. PATRICIA S. TANNER

Welcome to the Faith Clinic: Stress Edition — where we don't hand you cute verses and clichés. We hand you spiritual prescriptions for real pressure, real panic, and real prayers from tired believers holding it together by a thread.

This book is for the overwhelmed—those trusting God while juggling bills, burnout, hustle culture, and holy frustration. If you've ever whispered, "God, are You even watching this mess?" this is for you.

Inside you'll find raw, soul-hitting chapters like:

- "God, I Trust You — But These Bills Keep Coming"
- "If Rest Is Holy, Why Does It Feel Like Slacking?"
- "I'm Tired of Smiling So You Won't Worry"

This isn't fluff. It's real talk for real stress—and a reminder that you're not forgotten, you're being fortified.

The Faith Clinic is open. Breathe in & take your spiritual vitamins. Healing begins here.

NOW AVAILABLE:
www.amazon.com

FAITH CLINIC-VOLUME VI-GRIEF CLINIC EDITION

This isn't just a feeling — it's a flare signal from the soul. You pray, serve, and believe in God, but something deep inside is still simmering. Welcome to the Faith Clinic: Anger Edition — where suppressed emotions meet sacred intervention.

In this volume, Dr. Patricia S. Tanner guides you through spiritual triage for:

- ☑ Silent rage and emotional suppression
- ☑ The grief–anger connection
- ☑ Rejection wounds from childhood to church hurt

This isn't a lecture. It's a spiritual detox. No shame. No sugar-coating. Just raw, honest healing. Whether you're snapping at loved ones or silently seething under the surface, this book meets you at the boiling point—and leads you to the breakthrough.

- ⚕ This is the clinic.
- 💧 This is your moment.

And God is ready to heal the anger behind your amen.

NOW AVAILABLE:
www.amazon.com

DR. PATRICIA S. TANNER

30 Days Of Grieving

Given By The Inspiration Of God

Healing From COVID-19

Almost a year later, it hit me... My mother was gone, and I was still stuck at the hospital. I had tried everything from crying to counseling, and even prayer. Pray they told me. Trust God they insisted. But it seemed as if nothing was working. I was hurt, dealing with my reality: my mother was not coming back.

While journeying through grief, it was under the divine 'Inspiration of God' that He placed me in a trance. While I was gaining a revelation about grief, He gave me this journal, '30 Days Of Grieving.'

NOW AVAILABLE:
www.amazon.com

FAITH CLINIC-VOLUME VI-GRIEF CLINIC EDITION

The 30 Days Challenge:
I Tested POSITIVE for COVID-19

If you had 30 days to live, what would you do? If you were told that you needed to prepare for a marathon in 30 days and you were completely out of shape, what would you do first? If a family member handed you one million dollars and told you that you had to figure out how to build a house (debt free), how would you execute your plan?

I'm catching you off guard with these requests, right? Well, this is exactly what COVID-19 did when it snatched my mother's life away, wrecking my entire world. I had to battle for my mother AND my faith in 30 days flat. What a challenge!

Throughout this book, I will walk you through my brief journey with COVID-19, negative of a happy ending. I will share the diary I kept while attending to my mother, and the scriptures I read, prayed, and quoted as my shield and protection.

Take the journey with me, there is healing on the other side!

NOW AVAILABLE:
www.amazon.com

DR. PATRICIA S. TANNER

Can Salvation Get You Into Heaven? The Answer Is Yes! offers a powerful and biblically grounded exploration of God's eternal plan, revealing the heart of the Gospel and the assurance of salvation through Jesus Christ.

 Unpacking life's most vital questions—Who is God? Why were we created? What does Jesus' life mean for us?—this book brings clarity to the believer's journey and confirms that salvation, once received, is eternally secure.

Whether you're seeking understanding or affirming your faith, this inspiring guide will lead you into the confidence and joy of knowing heaven is your eternal home.

NOW AVAILABLE:
www.amazon.com

FAITH CLINIC-VOLUME VI-GRIEF CLINIC EDITION

The Bench That Waited is a bold and prophetic call to action for believers who've grown comfortable in church attendance but stagnant in purpose.

With raw honesty and spiritual insight, Patricia Tanner exposes the quiet crisis of passive faith—where callings are delayed and obedience is optional.

Through Scripture, stories, and reflection, this book urges readers to rise from routine, break free from spiritual stagnation, and step boldly into their Kingdom assignment. The bench has waited long enough—will you?

NOW AVAILABLE:
www.amazon.com

DR. PATRICIA S. TANNER

What happens when the Kingdom becomes a stranger?

The Godless Climb is not a rejection of faith—it is a raw, unflinching journey through what remains when belief unravels. With brutal honesty and tender grace, this book explores the spiritual free fall that follows the loss of divine certainty, the ache of unanswered prayers, and the void left when God no longer feels near.

Written for those who have quietly slipped out of the pews and into a wilderness of doubt, grief, and inner searching, this is not a triumph story—but a survival story. A confession. A sacred wrestle. Through personal reflection and prophetic insight, the author unpacks what it means to climb without a safety net, to live without the scaffolding of religious performance, and to build a new compass in the absence of old crutches.

You haven't arrived. But you're still climbing. And that is holy.

NOW AVAILABLE:
www.amazon.com

FAITH CLINIC-VOLUME VI-GRIEF CLINIC EDITION

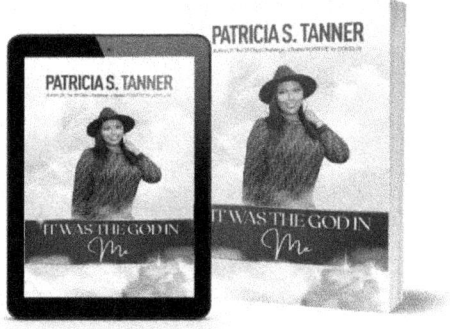

It Was The God In Me

Success can be attributed to many things. Depending on the person who has obtained success would determine those to whom they attribute their success. Some give credit to their daily routine while others give credit to a mentor or some sort of system they followed. When I think about my success, the only person who I can give the credit to is God.

In this memoir, I share the successes and failures I have experienced throughout my life. From my individual experiences to my entrepreneurial journey, I share how God has walked with me every step of the way.

Come and see.. It Was The God In Me!!

NOW AVAILABLE:
www.amazon.com

DR. PATRICIA S. TANNER

The Triple 7 Formula is designed for business owners who are looking forward to hitting the million-dollar mark in their business. If you own a business and seem to be running in financial circles, this book will get you on track to simultaneously gaining sound business structure and millions in your bank account.

It was through many conversations with business owners lacking financial gain that prompted Patricia to share her blueprint for millionaire status. Through this book, she demonstrates how to gain financial ground by developing strong teams, implementing systems, and setting stackable goals. If you are ready to gain a laser sharp focus, and implement these clear steps, you will position yourself for financial greatness. Your business will be sound, and you will see financial growth beyond your wildest dreams!!

NOW AVAILABLE:
www.amazon.com

The Triple 7 Formula is specifically crafted for business owners aspiring to reach the million-dollar milestone. If you are a business owner feeling stuck in financial cycles, this book will set you on the path to building both a solid business structure and financial success.

This workbook is designed to complement the textbook of the same name. As you progress through its pages, you will be inspired to take decisive steps toward becoming a millionaire. From constructing your business framework to creating the millionaire's avatar, this process will expand your knowledge and mindset. Not only will you chart a course to financial success, but you will also identify your accountability circle and select a mentor to guide you toward greatness.

I cannot guarantee millionaire status unless you actively follow the steps to begin your journey. If you are searching for a get rich quick scheme, this workbook is not for you. I am looking for those ready to put in the effort—and since you are reading this, I believe that's you!

You have finally found it: Your roadmap to millions!

NOW AVAILABLE:
WWW.Amazon.com

DR. PATRICIA S. TANNER

Find Patricia on The Web:

www.PatriciaTanner.com

Follow Patricia on social media:

Facebook & Instagram: @PatriciaTannerInc

DR. PATRICIA S. TANNER

www.ingramcontent.com/pod-product-compliance
Lightning Source LLC
Chambersburg PA
CBHW062221080426
42734CB00010B/1979